INTENSIVE CARE
Selected and New Poems

FIELD Translation Series 22

Miroslav Holub

INTENSIVE CARE:

Selected and New Poems

FIELD Translation Series 22
Oberlin College Press

ACKNOWLEDGMENTS

The translations by George Theiner were first pub-
lished by Penguin (Modern European Poets, 1967),
and we are grateful for permission to reprint them.

Translations by Ian and Jarmila Milner and by Ewald
Osers are from *Poems Before and After* (Bloodaxe,
1990), and we are grateful for permission to reprint
them.

Acknowledgment is also made to the following
periodicals, in which the new poems first appeared:
*California Anthology, Common Knowledge, FIELD,
Grand Street, International Quarterly, Island, New
Statesman, Partisan Review, Poetry Review, Prairie
Schooner, Times Literary Supplement, Trafika.*

Particular thanks go to Dana Hábová, for her pa-
tience, good spirits and ready helpfulness, over
many years.

Publication of this book was made possible in part
by a grant from the Ohio Arts Council.

Library of Congress Cataloging-in-Publication Data

Holub, Miroslav (translated by various hands)
   INTENSIVE CARE: Selected and New Poems
   (The FIELD Translation Series v. 22)

LC: 96-067483
ISBN: 0-932440-75-4
        0-932440-76-2 (paperback)

CONTENTS

A Note on the Selection and Translations

1. *(genealogy)*

Bones	13
Wings	14
Truth	15
The Door	16
Riders	17
Fall of Troy	18
Discobolos	19
The Fly	21
Napoleon	22
The Corporal Who Killed Archimedes	23
Great Ancestors	24
From the Travels of Abigdor Karo	25
Glass	26
Fish	27
Skinning	29
The Forest	32
Dreams	33
Five Minutes After the Air Raid	34
Annunciation	35
The Steam Car	36
The Prague of Jan Palach	37
Whaling	38
At Last	40
The Moth	41
Head-Smashed-In	42
Crowd-Walkers	43
The British Museum	44
The Ten Commandments	46
Supper	48

2. *(anthropology)*

Ode to Joy	51
Love	52
Lovers in August	53
Night at the Observatory	54
United Flight 412	55
Landscapes	56
The Minotaur on Love	57
On the Origin of 6 p.m.	59
Love, As They Say	61
Parallels Syndrome	62
The End of the Week	63
Freedom	64
The Day of the Pollyanna	65
The Dangers of the Night	66
Man Cursing the Sea	67
Burning	68
The Wall in the Corner by the Stairs	69
Half a Hedgehog	71
My Mother Learns Spanish	73
Autumn	74
Philosophy of Fall	75
The Garden of Old People	76
A Boy's Head	77
Prince Hamlet's Milk Tooth	78
Teacher	80
Hemophilia/Los Angeles	81
Immanuel Kant	83
Whale Songs	84
Elementary School Field Trip to the Dinosaur Exhibit	85
The Rampage	86
Masterpiece	88

3. *(semiology)*

Although	93
Swans in Flight	98
Teaching About Diseases	99

Brief Reflection on Cats Growing on Trees   100
Brief Reflection on Accuracy   102
Brief Reflection on the Theory of Relativity   104
Brief Reflection on an Old Woman with a
    Pushcart   105
Brief Reflection on Gargoyles   106
Brief Reflection on the Butchering of Carp   108
Brief Reflection on Floods   109
Meeting Ezra Pound   110
The Autumn Bus   111
The Angel of Death   113
Crucifix   117
Sand Game   120
Door II   123
Questioning   127
Fairy Tales   132
How We Played the Gilgamesh Epic   135
Scene with Fiddlers   139
Punch's Dream   140
The Sorcerer's Lament   141
Ganesha   142

4. *(pathology)*
Reality   145
Suffering   146
In the Microscope   149
Pathology   150
The Bomb   151
Explosion   152
The Dead   153
Collision   154
Brief Reflection on the Word 'Pain'   157
Distant Howling   158
Interferon   159
While Fleeing   165
The Earth is Shrinking   166
Spinal Cord   167
Heart Failure   168

Pompeii   171
Kuru, or the Smiling Death Syndrome   172
Vanishing Lung Syndrome   173
Crush Syndrome   174
Anencephaly   175
Intensive Care Unit   177
Heart Transplant   178

5. *(tautology)*
What Else   183
The Best Room, or Interpretation of a
    Poem   184
End of the Game   185
Landscape with Poets   187
Two in a Landscape   188
The Minotaur's Thoughts on Poetry   189
Conversation with a Poet   190
The Autumn Orchard   191
Literary Bash   192
The Pied Pipers   193
Anatomy of January   195
The Rain at Night   196
Fog   197
Behind the House   198
The Earliest Angels   199
Anything About God   200
The Statue of the Master   201
The Teaching of the Master   202
The Last Night Bus   203
The Bird   204
Spacetime   205

A Note on the Selection and Translations

This selection of new and previously published poems, including a number of prose poems and of what Holub calls his "Stage Poems," was made by the author, with consultation among his editors and translators.

The order, also determined by the author, is not chronological. Each section mixes new work with work from earlier collections, sometimes as far back as 1958, when Holub's first collection, *Day Duty*, was published.

The bulk of this collection consists of selections from three previous titles in the FIELD Translation Series:

Sagittal Section, 1980 (translated by Stuart Friebert and Dana Hábová)

Interferon, or On Theater, 1982 (translated by David Young and Dana Hábová)

Vanishing Lung Syndrome, 1990 (translated by David Young and Dana Hábová). The latter was also published simultaneously in the United Kingdom by Faber and Faber.

Many of the poems translated since have been the result of direct collaboration between the author and David Young.

Translators' credits follow each poem, with the following abbreviations:

GT: George Theiner
DH: Dana Hábová
SF: Stuart Friebert
DY: David Young
MH: Miroslav Holub
EO: Ewald Osers
IM/JM: Ian and Jarmila Milner

1
(genealogy)

Bones

We lay aside
   useless bones,
   ribs of reptiles,
   jawbones of cats,
   the hip-bone of the storm,
   the wish-bone of Fate.

   To prop the growing head
   of Man
We seek
   a backbone
   that will stay
   straight.

GT

Wings

We have
a map of the universe
for microbes,
we have
a map of a microbe
for the universe.

We have
a Grand Master of chess
made of electronic circuits.

But above all
we have
the ability
to sort peas,
to cup water in our hands,
to seek
the right screw
under the sofa
for hours

This
gives us
wings.

GT

Truth

He left, infallible, the door itself
                    was bruised as he
                    hit the mark.
We two sat awhile
                    the figures in the documents
                    staring at us like
                    green huge-headed beetles
                    out of the crevices of evening.
The books stretched
                    their spines,
the balance weighed just for the fun of it
                    and the glass beads in the necklace
                    of the god of sleep whispered
                    together in the scales.

'Have you ever been right?' one of us asked.
'I haven't.'

Then we counted on.
It was late
And outside the smoky town, frosty and purple,
   climbed to the stars.

GT

The Door

Go and open the door.
  Maybe outside there's
  a tree, or a wood,
  a garden,
  or a magic city.

Go and open the door.
  Maybe a dog's rummaging.
  Maybe you'll see a face,
or an eye,
or the picture
                of a picture.

Go and open the door.
  If there's a fog
  it will clear.

Go and open the door.
  Even if there's only
  the darkness ticking,
  even if there's only
  the hollow wind,
  even if
        nothing
                is there,
go and open the door.

At least
there'll be
a draught.

GT

Riders

Over the kind earth twisted like Christmas-bread
over the white earth inscribed grammatically

in nonpareil, brevier, pica,
over the wise earth resounding
like the skull of St Augustine,
over the earth smooth as satin
shrouding the bosom of mystery,

four riders are galloping
on plump white horses,
four rosy-cheeked riders with forget-me-not eyes,
with velvet hands,
with lyres, sugar-basins,
and classics,

one of them lectures,
another one makes love,
the third sings praises,
the fourth gazes into the distance.

The earth undulates slightly behind them,
like the skin of a water snake,
and in the marks of their hooves
grey smallpox erupts.

These will be
the four riders
of the Apocalypse.

GT

Fall of Troy

From burning Troy we took away
these rags of ours,
teeth in a glass
and a tattooed grandpa.

A bit further on the ancient quail
were nesting again
and silver pike were milting
in the quiet sky.

Nailed to the ground by a lance
a soldier
flapped a hand at us.
The wormwood spoke no word
nor did the gentian.

Just like home, said grandpa.

The bleating of lambs
arched a roof
over our heads.
The land flowed with manna.
From the time of the primary rocks
nothing had happened in fact.

And like a fingernail
grown into the flesh
our truth
was always with us.

We slept embraced,
rags wrapped about us,
teeth in a glass.
Just like home, said grandpa.

Nothing had happened in fact.
Only we understood
that Troy
            perhaps
                        had really
fallen.   *GT*

Discobolus

But
before his last throw
someone whispered from behind
     — Just a minute,
     we've got to talk this over --
     purely as a matter of form,
     — You don't know the set-up,
     buddy,

     OK, so you've got
     some initiative, but
     don't you get it

     — We've got to insist on
     total agreement
     for every throw,

he felt
the soft Sudanese reed
wind around his wrist,
he wanted to yell
but his mouth
was suddenly full
of the cotton candy of the night sky,

his muscles bulged
like Thessalian granite,
yet
there was really no point to it,
     — Keep moving,
     someone said,
     get out of the way, will you,

     Demosthenes'
     turn now,
and Demosthenes
took a grain of sand from under his tongue
and neatly
flicked it in his eye,

— Hurrah, one more
world record,
they shouted;

beside himself, in a fury, stripped of his name,
Discobolus
swung down from
his knees again
but he was
stone by now
and saw
just a single
huge grain of sand
from horizon to horizon.

So he just stood there.

And round the corner
the first school buses
led
by the best pedagogues
who referred mostly
to the play of shoulders,
the great big human heart
and the proud step forward
on the way to eternity.

SF/DH

The Fly

She sat on the willow bark
watching
part of the battle of Crécy,
the shrieks,
the moans,
the wails,
the trampling and tumbling.

During the fourteenth charge
of the French cavalry
she mated
with a brown-eyed male fly
from Vadincourt.

She rubbed her legs together
sitting on a disemboweled horse
meditating
on the immortality of flies.

Relieved she alighted
on the blue tongue
of the Duke of Clervaux.

When silence settled
and the whisper of decay
softly circled the bodies

and just
a few arms and legs
twitched under the trees,

she began to lay her eggs
on the single eye
of Johann Uhr,
the Royal Armorer.

And so it came to pass —
she was eaten by a swift
fleeing
from the fires of Estrés.

SF/DH

Napoleon

Children, when was
Napoleon Bonaparte born,
asks teacher.

A thousand years ago, the children say.
A hundred years ago, the children say.
Last year, the children say.
No one knows.

Children, what did
Napoleon Bonaparte do,
asks teacher.

Won a war, the children say.
Lost a war, the children say.
No one knows.

Our butcher had a dog
called Napoleon,
says František.
The butcher used to beat him and the dog died
of hunger
a year ago.

And all the children are now sorry
for Napoleon.

IM/JM

The Corporal Who Killed Archimedes

With one bold stroke
he killed the circle, tangent
and point of intersection
of parallels
in infinity.

On penalty
of quartering
he banned numbers
from three up.

Now in Syracuse
he leads a school of philosophers,
for another thousand years
squats on his halberd
and writes:

one   two
one   two
one   two
one   two

SF/DH

Great Ancestors

At night
their silhouettes are outlined
against the empty sky
like a squadron of Trojan horses.
Their whispers rise from wells
of apparently living water.

But when day breaks
the way an egg cracks
and full-grown men with truncheons are born,
and mothers bleed profoundly,

they turn into butterflies
with cabbage leaves for wings,
to jelly condensed from fog
in fading, babyish outlines,

their barely discernible hands
shake,

they forget to breathe,
and are afraid to speak a single
intelligible word.

Anyway,
we've picked up more genes from viruses
than from them.

They have no strength.
And we must be the strength of those
who have no strength.

DY/DH

From the Travels of Abigdor Karo*

That land
is marked by
a multitude of crosses,
large and small,
at crossroads,
along highways,
on a stone or on a tree,
in the far corners
of forests,
and minds,
and towns.

Jesus Christ
is on many of them.
Many are
still free.

DY/DH

*Karo was a sixteenth-century Jewish poet, the first historical per-
sonality buried in the Prague Jewish Cemetery.

Glass

Li Po was glass.
Kant was glass.

We observe ourselves like transparent
sea anemones.
We see the dark purple heart
beating,
we see the grey lungs, wings
rising and falling,
we see the oligochaetic
worms of thought
gnawing under the cap.

Linnaeus was glass.
Mozart was glass.
Franz Josef was glass.

In the transparent belly
we see the tubular moon,
and behind the crystalline mouth
the swallowed words.

A prisoner is glass,
a policeman is glass,
sixty glass robots
reside in the castle.

Behind the swallowed words
we see the glass-wool
of incessant melody.

Only the dead
draw the curtain
from within.

DY/DH

Fish

The Emperor Qin Shi-Huang-ti,
first supreme ruler of China,
reigned for nine months posthumously,
embalmed and seated
on his throne, surrounded
by piles of fish,
just in case
he might smell:

Blind eyes of fish, indulgent
moons of historiography,
fish-spawn, vowels
of the official loyalty oath,

swim-bladders of fish, shrines
of the true faith,
bloody fish-fins, ballots
voting to bury philosophers
alive,

naked little fish skulls, ritual
whispered chants of consent
to the stoning of those
who remember too much,

dried mucus of scales, zeal
of the ladies-in-waiting when Qin
merely rehearsed his immortality
in one of his twenty identical palaces,

fish-gills, safe conducts
good for all time,
fish-guts, the bitter
secrets of the state
where, in any case, sometimes
the emperor gets bumped off,

fish with a round ban against laughter
on their lips, fish, caryatids
with flesh falling off the bones,
fish, phosphorescent catalysts
of eternity,
fish, geniuses of muteness,

cartilaginous fish, bony fish,
little fish, big fish,
imperial fish
with the single distinctive function
of stinking clear up to here.

DY/DH

Skinning

We make a noose, tie it to the ladder or whatever,
pull the hind legs through and tighten the noose.
We cut the skin all around. It's easy.
    In the beginning the fact created the Word.
    And the Word hovered above the abyss.
    Then go your ways and I will be in your mouth
    and I will teach you what you should say.
And now we start skinning: we cut under the loins,
pull the skin over the genitals, tug it down
until the bony tail slips out
like the leg of a crab from the eighth millennium
when talk will no longer be necessary.

With both hands we grasp the bloody, sticky stuff
and pull it down towards the head with all our
    strength,
as if it were a straitjacket
for the fools of god,
revealing the silver nude,
the nymph from Lethe, hemorrhaging
in the muscles and fascias,
we pull it down towards the head
    and don't have to believe a thing because
meaning is lost with the connective tissue.
If necessary, we finish the cutting with a sharp knife
where words are joined too closely to the flesh,
and the skin slips down, we cut around the forelegs
push the joints through and break off
the paws, crack crack the first word, crack the last
    word,
from here up to the morning star, a rustling
of satin can be heard, as if
a blue sky was being torn into strips.

    There's nothing in the mind that wasn't
in the senses, and the subcutaneous tissue gives off
a mild stench, like distant smouldering cities.
Thus, working in silence we reach the head.
    And it's easy.

We stop at the neck, slip the fascia
along the jaw, sever the ears and pull them
over the head along with the whiskers, like a winter
    cap
dripping with lymph. Only a muscle
still twitches here and there.

On a framework of laths we stretch the skin
into the approximate shape of the body
and its semantics, the skin like
a pennant dotted with ruptured blood vessels
— the coat-of-arms of the last rabbit
on a blue field.

And the butcher is taught what he should say.

Already the first skinned rabbit
starts running on broken-boned limbs,
romping through fields and green pastures
that refresh him,
already hundreds of empty gray skins,
white scuts showing, run off to the black forests,
and thousands of naked bloody zombies
run into city streets
in mindless oblivion,
    meaningless, but
    deeply engaged in the meaningless,

skin here, bodies there,

yes Andrei, I am Goya, but
how do rotting rabbits concern Goya,
and what are empty skins to Spain,

this is the world of skins
and this the alternative world
of dripping muscles on bone, because
— we feel, with the butcher under the tongue —
the skinning is what matters here,
and it's so easy, Allen,
a skinned Moloch is even more
like a Moloch.

Keeping cool is the main thing.

The countryside with yellow flowers along the brook
where the flocks of empty gray skins
of little rabbits graze,
empty gray fur coats, twitching
their comical little skin noses,
empty skins communicating
by touching whiskers
with Diderot.

The royal capital, with gothic arcades,
where the naked rabbit bodies crowd together
under the lash of the pied pipers, bodies
raped by bodies, nakedness raped
by nakedness, in droll
hectic movements,

the Spanish gabble of the word
stripped of fact,
the drain of fact, left behind
by the word,
an empty Ferris wheel
swooping across the abyss
and towards the zenith.

And it all started
with a mere noose
and a ladder,
or whatever,
to heaven.

DY/DH

The Forest

Among the primary rocks
where the bird spirits
crack the granite seeds
and the tree statues
with their black arms
threaten the clouds,

suddenly
there comes a rumble,
as if history
were being uprooted,

the grass bristles,
boulders tremble,
the earth's surface cracks

and there grows

a mushroom,

immense as life itself,
filled with billions of cells
immense as life itself,
eternal,
watery,

appearing in this world for the first

and last time.

GT

Dreams

Taking sips from man
like the moon from dewdrops.
The rope grows straight up
from the crown of the head.
The black swan hatches
out of a pebble.
And a flock of angels in the sky
is taking an evening
skid-control course.

I am dreaming, therefore I am dreaming.
I am dreaming
that three times three is nine;
that there is a rule
of the right hand;
that when a circus leaves
the trampled arena
grows green with grass.

Yes, grass.
Grass with no double meaning.
Just grass.

DY/DH

Five Minutes After the Air Raid

In Pilsen,
Twenty-six Station Road,
she climbed to the Third Floor
up stairs which were all that was left
of the whole house,
she opened her door
full on to the sky,
stood gaping over the edge.

For this was the place
the world ended.

Then
she locked up carefully
lest someone steal
Sirius
or Aldebaran
from her kitchen,
went back downstairs
and settled herself
to wait
for the house to rise again
and for her husband to rise from the ashes
and for her children's hands and feet to be stuck
    back in place.

In the morning they found her
still as stone,
sparrows pecking her hands.

GT

Annunciation

It could be the erratic neighing of the night
outside, below the window,
when fire settles to sleep.
It could be the horns of Jericho,
it could be the choir hymn
    of hunchbacks underneath the snow,
it could be the oak speaking to willows,
it could be the chiffchaff hatching
    under the owl's wing.
It could be the archangel's decision,
and it could be the salamander's ominous prophecy.
It could be the weeping of our only love.

But the official slumped over his desk
turned to us and said:
Let us hearken: You must hearken.
You are expected to hearken.
Hearken more boldly,
boldly hearken more,
hearken, heark, he hearketh,
they hearken, more boldly,
we more boldly hearken,
hea rk en,
HEAR K EN,
HeaR k En Hear —
So we didn't hear a thing.

SF/DH

The Steam Car

When Josef Bozek, the inventor,
constructed his steam-driven
car, followed by his
steam-driven 'water boat,'
seven yards long,
he organized, 1 June 1817,
a public showing in Stromovka Park
for the high nobility
and the enlightened public
upon payment of an entrance fee.

Things had no sooner begun
than there was a sudden downpour
and in the resulting confusion
somebody stole the cash box
and the proceeds.

So that Bozek, the inventor,
lost all his money.

He demolished the steam car
with a sledgehammer.

Since that time
no steam-driven conveyances
have been seen in Bohemia.

The downpours
come frequently.

DY/DH

The Prague of Jan Palach

And here stomp Picasso's bulls.
And here march Dali's elephants on spidery legs.
And here beat Schönberg's drums.
And here rides Señor de la Mancha.
And here the Karamazovs are carrying Hamlet.
And here is the nucleus of the atom.
And here is the cosmodrome of the Moon.
And here stands a statue without the torch.
And here runs a torch without the statue.
And it's all so simple. Where
Man ends, the flame begins —
And in the ensuing silence can be heard the crumbling
of ash worms. For
those billions of people, taken by and large,
are keeping their traps shut.

GT

Whaling

There is a shortage of whales in some cities.
And yet, the whaling fleet cruises the streets.
A huge fleet in such a small town.
Or at least a harpoon creeps
from one sidewalk to the other,
and searches . . . and finds.
The house is pierced and in minute jerks
a weird creature quivers.
Minute blood soaks into the wall.

And that is the Old Testament plot,
the elementary drama,
the essential event,
to be pierced and dragged away,
between textbooks and copybooks,
    between algae and halibut,
between mummy's cups and pictures,
    between seaweed and cat's-paws,
between slippers and webs in the corner,
    between Morning star and Evening star,
to be pierced and dragged to glorify
the gods of piercing and dragging,
to be pierced and dragged to eternity,
in the stifling inner bellowing of blood,
wanting to remain and with convulsing claws
clutching the water drop on the tap,
reflections in the window pane,
the first baby hairs
    and fins.

But there is nothing but waves, waves, waves
and the undoing
of that nameless other shore,
with nothing good or bad,
just the arcuation of bones,
The scraping of plaster under which come to light
still older and older medieval frescoes,
The sloughing of skins under which stands out
the sliminess of the fetus just conceived.

And the maledictory unison of pipes is heard,
the music of whalers,
the fugue towering over one place
like an obelisk of the last breath
behind the curtains.

Nobody ever wrote
Antigone of whales, Electra of whales,
Hamlet of whales, Godot of whales,
Snow White of whales, not even
one flew over the whale's nest,

although the whale as such
is a sort of a metaphor.

Metaphors die out
in a situation which is a metaphor.
And whales die out
in a situation which is a killer whale.

SF/DH

At Last

At last we were masters of our heads,
masters of the city,
masters of our shadows
and our equinox.

Someone fired a shot to celebrate,
but only the kind with a cork
tied to a string.

And then we opened the cages
and ferrets ran out.
Out of the skull ran brown and white
spotted rats.
Out of the heart flew
blood-soaked cuckoos.

Out of the lungs
a condor rose, wheezing with rage
because of the way his plumes were squashed
in the bronchi.

Even a panther showed up,
on the loose from an obsolete circus,
starved, ready to eat
even a Claudius.

You could hear squeaks in the streets,
the groans and shouts
of extinguishing fiends.

And at last we are masters
of our new moon.

But we can't step out
of our doorways;
someone might cast
a spell on us.

We might even
be hostage
to ourselves.   *DY/MH*

The Moth

The moth
having left its pupa
in the galaxy of flour grains
and pots of rancid
drippings,

the moth
discovers in this
topical darkness
that it's a kind of butterfly
but
it can't believe it,
it can't believe it,

it can't believe
that it's a tiny,
flying, relatively
free moth

and it wants to go back,
but there's no way.

Freedom makes
the moth tremble
forever, that is,
twenty-two hours.

DY/DH

Head-Smashed-In

Orpheus touches the strings of his lyre,
the leopard lies down with the lamb,
the hare with the wolf,
narwhal with herring,
Eurydice wades gratuitously
with silver lamé ankles
in the nebulous endothelium
of heart vessels,
all of this rendered
in drypoint etchings or aquatints —
life's great unity

and

the United Nations has designated
the cliff in Alberta called Head-Smashed-In
as a World Cultural Heritage Site,
the cliff where, for six thousand years,
Indians stampeded buffalo herds
into the gorge
and finished them off at the bottom
(the bloody mass of hides,
horror, hoofs and horns,
roaring and bulging eye-balls),
in order to have enough meat.

So that

for six thousand years
Orpheus bangs the strings,
blood coagulates,
brain tissue softens and splinters,
the world cultural heritage
emanates sweet odors,
hysterics cluster at the altars

and

the heads and buffaloes
are still smashed-in.

DY/MH

Crowd-Walkers

That's how it goes.
The crowd-walker has arrived,
making his way on the heads of the masses,
his wooden steps echoing on their skulls,
and already the shaking hands
pour out from their sleeves,
from two, seven, thirty sleeves,
broken necks crawl out of collars,
the bacchants grow luminescent,
words are shredded on mute sandpaper,
blook soaks into socks.

He arrives like a bull with ten testes,
like a muscular mighty moleworm
shining with silvery mucus,
and we know no spells
against moleworms.
And in our heads, spermias
of all future crowd-walkers echo.

That's how it goes.
Because man's no career.
Moleworms are.

DY/MH

The British Museum

To the tune of "Bolero,"
any ark
will be ruined
once, the trilingual
Rosetta Stone will be broken, steles of Halicarnassus
will turn to dust, sandstone Assyrian spirits
with eagle heads will shyly take off,
the carved man-head lions of Ashursirpolis will croak,
the last red-granite hand of the Colossus of Thebes
will drop off, the Indian supergod Harikaru
will cover his onyx eyes, the Rhind mathematical
    scrolls
will catch fire, the suspended Zen poems will
    evaporate,
and the green hellish judge from the Ming dynasty
    will whine.

For the time of stone is meted out
and so is the time of myth.

Only genes are eternal,
from body to body,
from one breed to another breed,
on Southampton Row
in fact
you find walking genetic codes of Egyptian mummies,
deoxyribonucleic acid of the man from Gebelin,
hereditary traits of the man from Lindow,
whose bodily receptacle, cut in half by a bulldozer,
successfully swells under a glass bell,
in Bloomsbury, in fact, you find
all the eternity of the world rushing around
buying black flowers
for the Last Judgment, less Last
than a midnight hotdog.

So the British Museum is not to be found
in the British Museum.

The British Museum is in us,
quite in the middle,
quite at the bottom.

DY/DH

The Ten Commandments

And what are these commandments
right here, right now?

Moses in the form of an old drug addict
with a massive sticky beard,
the whole body changed into soul, but it stinks
a little,
his overcoat like a Babylonian dung heap,
he sleeps in the morning rays of the leftover sun
in the portal of a theater on the Strand,
dreams like rolls of barbed wire,
zippered-up dreams, like the mating of centipedes,
dreams like wings growing on man
just before the abyss,

like when you turn off the computer and forget
to put it into the memory,
like when the Lord of multitudes
flees the multitudes.

All the wisdom of the world is in his bag, worn
as the stomach wall of a camel from Canaan,
like the dura mater of an anencephalos,
hundreds of frayed rolls
of old newspapers held with rubber bands,
everything that happened over the last ten years
set in the alphabet of the dermestes beetles.

And what are these commandments,
one should ask Moses, the ram with curly horns,
stinking at the head of the herd, at the portal of the
    theater,

and he is (silently) asked by thousands of
    mid-morning sheep,
chewing, scribbled over with eight-point type,
sexual sheep of foam rubber,
commercial sheep of brown polyethylene,
lambs of frayed denim,
tourist lambs with Baedeker erections,
apostolic herd of mutton with azure-blue parasols,

coming down in four-cycle chariots
from heaven, greased with Johnson's wax.

And he is going to preach the ten commandments
   ten times for ten pence,
the ten commandments as ten mutations of the virus
of immunodeficiency,
as ten gulps from a goatskin bag,
with the last breath.

And in fact the ten commandments will be
ten times why — and therefore for nothing
at the very end of the magnetic tape
stretching along an inclined plane
around the world
and back.

DY/DH

Supper

You must eat all your soup, that's how you get
    strong.
Eat that soupie, stop playing with it!
Or else you'll be weak and you won't grow up.
And that'll be your fault.
If it comes to that, towns and nations are to blame
    when they don't grow up.
I blame small towns for not becoming cities. Their
    tough luck.
I blame little nations for not growing powerful.
    Their tough luck.
Accuso le piccole nazioni . . .
Ich beschuldige die kleinen Nationen . . .
J'accuse les petites nations . . .
So bolt that soup, before it turns to ice!

SF/DH

2
(anthropology)

Ode to Joy

You only love
when you love in vain.

Try another radio probe
when ten have failed,
take two hundred rabbits
when a hundred have died:
only this is science.

You ask the secret.
It has just one name:
again.

In the end
a dog carries in his jaws
his image in the water,
people rivet the new moon,
I love you.

Like caryatids
our lifted arms
hold up time's granite load

and defeated
we shall always win.

GT

Love

Two thousand cigarettes.
A hundred miles
from wall to wall.
An eternity and a half of vigils
blanker than snow.

Tons of words
old as the tracks
of a platypus in the sand.

A hundred books we didn't write.
A hundred pyramids we didn't build.

Sweepings.
Dust.

Bitter
as the beginning of the world.

Believe me when I say
it was beautiful.

GT

Lovers in August

Your hand travelled
   the Aztec trail
   down my breast.
The sun popped out like the egg
   of a platypus
and aspens pattered
   their leafy Ur-language.
All this has happened before.

The jellied landscape
   was furrowed with happiness.
You worshipped me
   like the goddess of warm rain.

But in each corner of our eyes
   stood one of Maxwell's demons
loosening the molecules
   of rise and fall
back and forth.

And in and out, round and about,
   in and out,
through the cracked lens of the eye
   unendingly,
   surface behind glass
   entropy mounted
   in the random and senseless universe.

All this has happened before.
All this will happen again.

GT

Night at the Observatory

It was thawing.
As if the Avars
were attacking underground.

They stood leaning in the shadows,
his finger discovered
an inch
of unknown gentle country
beneath her left shoulder,

Atlantis, he said,
Atlantis.

Above the fields the wires hissed like iguanas.
A car's horn faded on the air
like a voice from Greek tragedy.
Behind the walls the guard paced back and forth.
Hares were sniffing the distant town.
Wood rotted in the ground.
The Avars were winning.
Trees cracked at the joints.
The wind came and veered off.
They kissed.

From somewhere a rock was falling
its second thousand years.
And the stars were taking in
signals on a frequency of ten megacycles,
beamed to a civilization
which had died
just before the dawn
of eternity.

GT

United Flight 412

Megalopolis far behind,
overwhelmed by air. Left over:
a few towers, the rumbling crowds,
the shells on Oceanside Beach
and the gentle yielding of your body
in the atmospheric turbulence
                                        called morning.

Thirty thousand feet high
you answered, yes,
I love you, yes.
The Fasten Seat Belts sign came on
and the 727
was set for a smooth landing.

In principle, of course, it was fixed
in the immense white box of sky
like a butterfly
on the pin of a word.

Because where would we be
if love was not stronger than poetry
and poetry stronger than love?

DY/DH

Landscapes

Yes, you were there, Helen. We were supposed to be
picking beets, but the inebriated veterinarian kept
throwing them at us, and we had to duck as they
whistled past our ears. And he kept asking you to
have schnapps with him. Mud mixed with hate. The
photographer fell in the brook and got badly bruised.
An ambulance was on the way.

But it was peaceful in the distance.
Far in the north, on the ridge,
a fine smoke. Somebody barbecuing somebody.

Far in the west
hunters gathered,
fat as possums. Their jaws

were set to devour the mammals and birds
and pull the whole horizon
out of kilter.

Far in the south —
clouds copulating in grays
and a lightning bolt shaped like a tree
stuck in the earth.

Then the farm officials came and got mad because the
beets were all over the place. Everyone else was drunk,
so they got mad at us.

On the hedge, next to the mousehole,
a butterbur bloomed, confused
by this autumn spectacle,
although it was all
perfectly obvious.

DY/DH

The Minotaur on Love

The love of the Centaurs is eternal
like being broken on the wheel.

That night, however, when Ariadne
gave Theseus that fateful thread
(and I could see them, for the labyrinth's walls
recede and open at the equinox)
(and I could see them, for I was Theseus
just as Theseus
can be me)
that night they faced each other
and his hands rested
upon her shoulders:

their features were dark
as the waves of the Styx and
their bodies were of stone.
They stood and up above them stood the moon
and stood the sea.
And it was clear that love is not
in movements but
in a kind of menacing
endurance that escapes from time.

At length they turned transparent and
the worms could be seen gnawing
deep within them: she knew then
that she would die on Naxos
and queue for olives as if that
were the meaning of life,
he knew that he would die in Athens,
a king of the theatre
with ten mistresses
and cirrhosis of the liver.

But then they stood, his hands upon her shoulders,
and up above them stood the moon
and there stood the sea. And I,
faced with that love,
I dug my bull's head
into the sand and in some unfamiliar

despair I smashed the walls
and roared O Theseus, Theseus,
I'm waiting for you, Theseus,
and then the labyrinth flung back at me the words
and my own
Homeric laughter.

EO

On the Origin of 6 p.m.

Human fates are
simplified by names.

The day, gnawed by the sun,
tossed among the dummy houses:
we walk, dragging our love behind us
like a big croaked dog.
>   But how many lives have been saved
>   by mouth-to-mouth resuscitation?

And that is all, that vacuum-sealed vanity?
That talk of herrings in an undated tin?
Certainly. And we hold our fork
in the left hand and put the bones
on the side of the plate, for eternity.
>   Your eyes, of course, are neon
>   and wherever you look a fiery
>   writing appears on the wall.

There are no words. There never were
when it came to the crunch. On the threshold of fate
poetry is silent, choked
by its own bitterness.
>   Fortunately I hardly ever
>   understand you.

We write upon each other with scalpels,
like a Chinese poet drawing with a brush.
Some blood coagulates quickly,
some flows and flows.
>   The magnitude of things
>   is measured by the depth of the cut.

We cross on the red light. Because the game
is without rules, and many years ago
they plundered our chessboard squares,
so nothing but the snoring of the kings remains,
and shouts of pawns and neighing of knights' horses:
and on all these we are enjoined to silence.
>   But when I kiss you
>   your tongue tastes
>   of a tenth planet, a parthenogenetic one.

And that is all, that claw of darkness?
These suicides of sleep, from which
we awake right under the stone?
And that is all, that examination
of skeletal remains?
    Your gait indeed is royal:
    frightening infallibility of breasts.
    You walk without motion.

We live by hope. Certainly. Its
parasites gnaw in the brain's emulsion.
A latent image is left.
Sometimes not even that.

And so it's six o'clock
this day. The same as yesterday.
The same as tomorrow.

EO

Love, As They Say

Days and nights take turns, minute after minute.
Central Park turns round,
the collector jumps on the platform
of the merry-go-round and collects
tickets from water-nymphs and horses.
That doesn't concern us.

Behind glass, stick insects mate,
and she is devouring his head,
he doesn't need it for mating anyway.

The key fits in the lock,
a molecule fits in a molecule,
John the Baptist baptizes as always,
looking away.

For us, the Exodus from Egypt
begins again. For us this is
the advent of invisibility,
the night of glowing strawberries,
the sepia darkness undersea
with a single warm tentacle.

For us, this is the cover
of a book without letters or pictures,
the contents to follow later,
it is — as always — for the first time in history,
for the last time in the history of skin,
the last time in the history of parchment,
like the tale of the unborn swineherds,
the under-the-altar sacrament, still unknown,
with the light of eternity
turned all the way up.

This is the only extraterrestrial thing
left to us.

Like the victorious palpitation of silky wings
on the temporary tombs of butterflies.
And of stick insects with chitinous vaginas.

DY/DH

Parallels Syndrome

Two parallels
always meet
when we draw them ourselves.

The question is,
ahead
or behind us.

Whether the train in the distance
is coming
or going.

DY/DH

The End of the Week

Of course it's all based
on a timetable, sometimes valid
Monday to Friday, sometimes on Saturday,
very rarely on Sunday (when He rested
from all His labors),

and we carry it in a forgotten pocket
so we usually miss the train.

But we'll get there anyway.

It will be Sunday again, the day of withered songs.
On the first floor, by the window without curtains,
a little girl in a red dress will stand
and wait.

In the Spanish square they'll be burning
eighteen Jewish marranos
in honor of the wedding of Maria Luisa and Carlos,

But we won't even stop
and will go home the back way,
deep in thought.

DY/DH

Freedom

At a dizzying height
on the skyscraper's wall
a sky-blue flag.

    Down the middle of the street
    a polio-stricken boy
    on roller-skates
    passes spasmodically,

        pushing himself ahead
        with just one foot,
        the one that isn't
        artificial.

DY/MH

The Day of the Pollyanna

The dough didn't rise that day.
The kitchen clock stopped.
Against all hope
the streetcar turned around
at the Slovany terminal
and started back.

But in the second car,
in the very back, a little girl
wearing a big blue woolen cap,
sat holding a doll
that resembled a three-month-old
tapir fetus,
singing, in a tinny voice,

Don't cry . . . don't cry . . . don't cry.

Though nobody felt like crying,
tapirs least of all.

DY/DH

The Dangers of the Night

Bedroom; a double bed; ceiling; bedside table; radio.
And outside darkness propped up by the trees
beneath which a dark blue jaguar is prowling.

The walls part and the double helix
of oneness
pervades the shadowy breathing of the roof.

Perhaps a galaxy. But more probably
the whites of eyes giving a hint of wind.

The enemy is approaching: the black image,
the image of oneself
in the mirror, sleep. His hands
are growing and his fingertips are
touching.

Resist. For in the morning,
in the naive light of songbirds' brains,
he that wakes will be
someone else.

EO

Man Cursing the Sea

Someone
just climbed to the top of the cliffs
and began to curse the sea.

Dumb water, stupid pregnant water,
slow, slimy copy of the sky,
you peddler between sun and moon,
pettifogging pawnbroker of shells,
soluble, loud-mouthed bull,
fertilizing the rocks with your blood,
suicidal sword
dashed to bits on the headland,
hydra, hydrolyzing the night,
breathing salty clouds of silence,
spreading jelly wings
in vain, in vain,
gorgon, devouring its own body,

water, you absurd flat skull of water —

And so he cursed the sea for a spell,
it licked his footprints in the sand
like a wounded dog.

And then he came down
and patted
the tiny immense stormy mirror of the sea.

There you go, water, he said,
and went his way.

SF/DH

Burning

The fire was creeping along the logs,
whispering curses and weaving spells.
Then it settled into a corner
and began to grow and sing.
It found its speech
in an old letter
from mother.

Orestes' fire. Antigone's fire.
The terrible fire; it's hot
and the black human smoke
rises toward heaven.

DY/DH

The Wall in the Corner by the Stairs

The wall
covered with the stucco
of oblivion,
a bit slanted,
somewhat invisible
in the glassy eye
of the mundane.

Coarse plaster,
a vertical burying ground of rhizopods,
grains of sand
of Mathias Braun, sculptor and Baroque painter, and
husks of Celtic germs.

A thin latex coating and a cobweb,
a laurel wreath
on the neck of last year's gnat
trembling in the draft
like a mummy of our
forever distant
love for Helen of Troy.

A crack like
a dried-up barge-puller's river,
a hole left by a nail,
the mouth of the volcano
Empedocles jumped into,
big as a sigh,
the hollow brain of a mite,
the little mouth of a prince
open in wonder
at the dry-handedness
of our memory.

Paintings on walls.
A framed Saroyan. A framed Beckett.
A framed Breughel.
Mummy, when she was twenty, framed,
me, when I was six, framed,

all
dead
for ages.

All identical with the wall.

DY/DH

Half a Hedgehog

The rear half was run over,
leaving the head, thorax,
and two front hedgehog legs intact.

A scream, cramping the mouth
open: the scream of mutes,
more horrible than the silence after a flood,
when even black swans
swim belly up.

And even if a hedgehog doctor
could be found in a hollow stump,
under leaves in a stand of oaks,
it would be no help
to a mere half, here on Route E 12.

In the name of logic,
in the name of teachings on pain,
in the name of hedgehog god the father,
the son and the holy ghost amen,
in the name of children's games and unripe berries,
in the name of fast creeks of love,
always different and always bloody,
in the name of roots that grow
over the stillborn baby's head,
in the name of satanic beauty,
in the name of fresh-dressed human skin,
in the name of all halves
and double helices, purines
and pyrimidines

we tried to run over
the hedgehog's head with the front wheel.

This was like operating
a lunar module from a planetary distance,
from a control center seized
by a cataleptic sleep.

And the mission failed. I got out
and found a heavy piece of brick.

Half a hedgehog cried on. And now
the crying became speech

resounding from the ceilings of our graves:

*And then comes death
and he will have your eyes.*

DY/DH

My Mother Learns Spanish

She started at the age
of eighty-two. She falls asleep
each time, page 26.
Algo se trama.

The pencil that underlines verbs
sets out on the page reluctantly
tracing the delicate outlines
of death.
No hay necesidad de respuestas.

It draws the routes
of Hernan Cortez's errands.
It draws El Greco's eye.
It draws Picasso's fish,
too big for its own aquarium.

A pencil as stubborn
as Fuente Ovejuna.
As the bull in the arena
Placa de Toros Monumental,
already on its knees
while horses wait
to drag away its body.

No hay necesidad de respuestas,
no answers are needed.
Now or ever.
She sleeps
ever now.

While Gaudi
as if in homage
never completes
his cathedral,
Sagrada Familia.

DY/MH

Autumn

And it is all over.

No more sweetpeas,
no more wide-eyed bunnies
dropping from the sky.

Only
a reddish boniness
under the sun of hoarfrost,
a thievish fog,
an insipid solution of love,
                    hate
                    and crowing.

But next year
larches will try
to make the land full of larches again
and larks will try
to make the land full of larks.

And thrushes will try
to make all the trees sing,
and goldfinches will try
to make all the grass golden,

and burying beetles
with their creaky love will try
to make all the corpses
rise from the dead,

Amen.

SF/DH

Philosophy of Fall

Fingers of the autumn sun
fiddle with yellow foliage
outside. The window reflects
a book and a silhouette
and a silhouette, a halo of hair,
this year we are
immersed in history
like a web in light.

I'm asking whether the existing
lack of genius
is caused by the elimination
of tertiary stages of syphilis.

Some God's spider
hovering above you, above me,
and above the Alka Seltzer.

SF/DH

The Garden of Old People

Malignant growth of ivy.
And unkempt grass,
it makes no difference now.
Under the trees, the invasion
of the fruit-bearing Gothic.
Darkness set in, mythological
and toothless.

But Minotaurus beat it
through a hole in the fence.
Somewhere, Icaruses
got stuck in webs.

On a bright early morning
the bushes reveal
the unabashedly gray, impudent
frontal bone of fact.
Gaping without a word.

SF/DH

A Boy's Head

In it there is a space-ship
and a project
for doing away with piano lessons.

And there is
Noah's ark,
which shall be first.

And there is
an entirely new bird,
an entirely new hare,
an entirely new bumble-bee.

There is a river
that flows upwards.

There is a multiplication table.

There is anti-matter.

And it just cannot be trimmed.

I believe
that only what cannot be trimmed
is a head.

There is much promise
in the circumstance
that so many people have heads.

GT

Prince Hamlet's Milk Tooth

His tooth fell out milky as
        a dandelion
and everything began to fall,
        as if a rosary had broken,
        or the string of time had snapped,
and it was downhill all the way;
round the corner the hearse driver gets up from
    supper,
his blind horse leading him, jolting along.
Hamlet, we're on our way.

No time now except hurry —
        learn to add and multiply,
        learn to cheat, whisper answers,
        smoke and make love,
        lay in stocks of permanganate
        and naphthalene,
there won't be any more.
And we're on our way, Hamlet.

At dusk you hear the drunken Danes making a
        racket
        and the pollinated flowers trampling around,
at dawn the typewriters tap out
        piles of loyalty checks
        with skeleton fingers,
at noon the paper tigers roar
        and committees count off races,
        what will be left for seed
        when it's all over?
Hamlet, we're on our way.

But we'll put a bird on our heads
        instead of a soldier's cap, won't we?
We'll walk through the park

        and in the shadow of a red rock
('come in under the shadow of this red rock')
        we'll learn
        to think it over
        in a small way,

the way moss grows,
the way sponges soak up water,
or we'll take a walk
five minutes out of town,
grow smaller and smaller,
a pacemaker over our hearts,
tuned to an easy rhythm

so the wolf has eaten, and the goat's still there,
we'll take the oath a little
and lie a little,
because not lying's in short supply,
brave lads, salt of the earth,
with our muddled hopes
one fine day
we'll damn well prove our salt,
Hamlet.

And keep that tooth of yours.
That's all there is.

SF/DH

Teacher

The Earth is turning,
    says the pupil.
No, the Earth is turning,
    says the teacher.

Thy leaf has perish'd in the green,
    says the pupil.
No, Thy leaf has perish'd in the green,
    says the teacher.

Two and two is four,
    says the pupil.
Two and two is four,
    the teacher corrects him.

Because the teacher knows better.

SF/DH

Hemophilia/Los Angeles

And so it circulates
from the San Bernardino Freeway
to the Santa Monica Freeway and
down to the San Diego Freeway and
up to the Golden State Freeway,

and so it circulates
in the vessels of the marine creature,
transparent creature,
unbelievable creature in the light
of the southern moon
like the footprint
of the last foot in the world,

and so it circulates
as if there were no other music
except Perpetual Motion,
as if there were no conductor
directing an orchestra of black angels
without a full score:

out of the grand piano floats
a pink C-sharp in the upper octave,
out of the violin
blood may trickle at any time,
and in the joints of the trombone
there swells a fear of the tiniest staccato,

as if there were no Dante
in a wheelchair,
holding a ball of cotton to his mouth,
afraid to speak a line
lest he perforate the meaning,

as if there were no genes
except the gene for defects
and emergency telephone calls,

and so it circulates
with the full, velvet hum of the disease,
circulates all hours of the day,

circulates all hours of the night
to the praise of non-clotting,

each blood cell carrying
four molecules of hope
that it might all be something
totally different
from what it is.

DY/DH

Immanuel Kant

The philosophy of white blood cells:
this is self,
this is non-self.
The starry sky of non-self,
perfectly mirrored
deep inside.
Immanuel Kant,
perfectly mirrored
deep inside.

And he knows nothing about it,
he is only afraid of drafts.
And he knows nothing about it,
though this is the critique
of pure reason.

Deep inside.

DY/DH

Whale Songs

At two o'clock in the morning
I hear my mitral valve
from the depth of the dim, blood-filled tunnel
which is me. Cellular receptors
fit with a metallic click into the locks
and the cells are me and the locks are me.
From some symphonic distance
there sounds the song of the whales,
and it contains me.

In some black castle
Sleeping Beauty has pricked herself on a thorn,
which is me. The clock has stopped
— in our house clocks stop any moment
because she pricks herself any moment,
on a tiny crock,
on a word,
on a milk tooth,
on a toy that fell into the gutter —
and so there's a still life, *nature morte*,
with me in the genetic background.

A paper kite stiffens in the air,
however, Einstein says, Time is always going, but
    never gone,
however, my mother says, ten years after her death,
Oh yes, oh yes,
and a clock starts again,
the Invisible passes through the room like a ball of
    lightning,
Sleeping Beauty lays eggs full of little spiders,
the whales re-enter the tunnel

and I start again
being the machine
for the production
of myself.

DY/MH

Elementary School Field Trip
to the Dinosaur Exhibit

Jurassic
roar.

Answered by
St. Georges
or Rambos.

Only one
glum little boy,
evidently blind,
is lifted to the Triceratops
to breathlessly run his hand
up and down the skull,
over the bony collar,
the horns above the eyes,
the skin-folds on the neck,

the boy's face
is insanely blank,
but the hand already knows
that nothing is in the mind
that hasn't been in the senses,
that giants are pinkish-gray
like Händel's Concerto Grosso
that life is just a step aside
just like mother
always said.

Triceratops,
Abel's younger brother.

Dark in there, in
the midbrain:
the last dinosaur
meeting the last man.

DY/MH

The Rampage

The last time
there was a genuine rampage,
herds stampeding
with the zest of hurricanes,
with the pulsations of a storm,
and the force of destiny,

when the roar went up
against the villous ceiling,
when the stronger ones
pushed forward to the cruel
thunder of whips while the zombies
fell back into permanent darkness,

the last time
when the cavalry charged
across the whole width of the enemy line
into the gap between life and death,
and not even one single droplet of misery
drizzled,

the last time
something really won
and the rest turned into compost

that was when the sperm
made the journey
up the oviduct.

That was a run for the money.

Since that time we've been tottering round
with the embarrassment of softening skeletons,
with the wistful caution
of mountain gorillas in the rain;
we keep hoping for the time-lapse soul,
we are secreting
marital problems and
a stationary home metaphysics.

against which
the adenosine triphosphate of every fucked-up cell
is like the explosion of a star
in a chicken coop.

DY/MH

Masterpiece

The only masterpiece
I ever created
was a picture of the moth Thysania agrippina
in pastel on gray paper.

Because I was never
much good at painting. The essence of art
is that we aren't very good at it.

The moth Thysania agrippina
rose from the stiff gray paper
with outstretched, comb-like antennae,

with a plush bottom resembling the buttocks
of the pigwidgeons of Hieronymus Bosch,
with thin legs on a shrunken chest
like those on Breughel's grotesque figures
in "Dulle Griet," it turned into Dulle Griet
with a bundle of pots and pans in her bony hand,

it turned into Bodhiddharma
with long sleeves,

it was Ying or Shade
and Yang or Light, Chwei or Darkness
and Ming or Glow, it had
the black color of water, the ochre color of earth,
the blue color of wood,

I was as proud of it as an Antwerp councilor
or the Tenth Patriarch from the Yellow River,

I sprinkled it with shellac, which is
the oath that painters swear on Goethe's Science of
    Colors,

and then the art teacher took it to his study

and I forgot all about it

the way Granny used to forget
her dentures in a glass.

DY/DH

3
(semiology)

Although

Although a poem arises when there's nothing else to be done, although a poem is a last attempt at order when one can't stand disorder any longer,

although poets are most needed when freedom, vitamin C, communications, laws and hypertension therapy are also most needed,

although to be an artist is to fail and art is fidelity to failure, as Samuel Beckett says,

a poem is not one of the last but one of the first things of man.

*

Although a poem is only a little word machine (as William Carlos Williams says) a little word machine ticking in the world of megamachines and megatons and megaelectronvolts,

although in the world of a poem one doesn't live any better than in any other world, although the world of a poem is dreary, arises out of desolation and perishes in the desolation of spiritual history,

although art doesn't solve problems but rather only wears them out, as Susan Sontag says,

yet a poem is the only sword and shield:

for in principle and essence it is not against tyrants, against automobiles, against madness and cancer and the gates of death, but against what is there all the time, all the time inside and out, all the time in front, behind, and in the middle, all the time with us and against us.

It is against emptiness. A poem is being, against emptiness. Against the primary and secondary emptiness.

*

The limits of emptiness: emptiness begins where the limits of man end. The limits of man as the principle of arranging and determining, seeing and conceiving a plan against the entropy of dead things. The limits of man expand and contract, pulse with his energy.

And emptiness is greatest where man was rather than where he was not. Interstellar space is not empty, but there is no worse emptiness than a house in ruins.

Or a thought that has come to nothing.

Observing the stars, we experience an emptiness which is not theirs.

*

Emptiness doesn't approach like a catastrophe or torrent. Emptiness seeps. Seeps through an unrepaired roof or a filthy desk. Emptiness seeps through cracks in roads and cracks in dreams. The master-key which opens emptiness is called I couldn't care less.

Emptiness is not knowledge of impotence but the demand for impotence. Admission of the claim to impotence. The will to impotence.

Emptiness is the drops we ourselves consider to be the flood which according to law is to come after us.

*

And emptiness is not the concern of the single person, of the isolated individual. By its aspect of disorderliness it becomes the affair of all, concretises itself as life environment, is inhaled, infects, multiplies, epidemicises.

Its focus is where there are no self-purifying forces of any stable inter-human order, where there is no relying either on history or ancient beauty or a new powerful image of life. Where things and thoughts depend entirely on new creation and a newly imprinted order and where there is no perfection in the new creation nor stability in the order.

*

I certainly don't think that our being is essence, the thing is to fill our being with essence; in that 'is to,' in that 'is necessary,' we actually are. Or I am.

But what a peculiar relationship exists between what is and what ought to be, between being and the fulfilment of being. A dream is what transcends existence and the dreamer. A dream is what ought to be. But with the first step towards a dream's fulfilment, its realisation and therefore transcendence, its content is no longer the mere expression of human freedom but a symptom of obligation. And obligations go very hard with us, though they are the fruits of our freedom: how exceptional it is to finish a book with the same feeling of perfection as that with which it was begun. How difficult it is to continue a friendship with the same purity as at the beginning. How difficult it is to finish building a shed with boards of the same size as the first two.

There is tension not only between reality and dream, but between dream and the realisation of dream.

And in stretched seams, emptiness arises.

Tension, which leads to fulfilment, continues above what is realised. Tension lasts and petrifies. Hardens. Becomes a stable sign and organ. It is no longer mere stimulus but also resignation.

And in hardened seams, emptiness arises.

*

We demand freedom also in regard to what we have freely chosen. But this freedom goes against itself. This freedom means confinement in the approximate, the impossible, the unreal; confinement in futility.

And is this what is human? Where does this feeling, and in the end conception, of the human come from? Of the human which exists in a self-contradicting freedom, in the freedom to betray our dreams and the beginnings of self-realisation, in the freedom to betray our order. In the freedom that goes against one of the few evidences of self-realisation, against the evidence of science in the broadest sense of the word.

This romantic human is not human, but a retreat from the human. It is not a fulfilment of being, but a regression to being without needs, without fulfilment, without essence.

*

Freedom is not the return to emptiness but fullness of being. Freedom is not regression from integration and determinacy but realisation of the higher forms of relatedness. And dependence. In the reverse case a new-born child would be more free than Beethoven or Comenius; and an opossum than a new-born child.

Freedom is the goal and therefore also the bond of culture and civilisation; the freedom that is sought in regression to the past conditions of mankind and men is a *contradictio in adiecto*: otherwise why did we take on all the wear and tear of humanising apes?

Freedom, as the search for higher forms of determining the human, certainly presupposes the fully developed consciousness of modern man, not the intoxicated sub-cortex of the human brain nor any unrestrained individuality foot-loose in the primal nature of lightning, putrefaction and termites, wild flowers and mating. Similarly we cannot manipulate the collective mind of citizens so that it fiddles with itself as it would with a TV set. Or with politics.

Freedom — so easily defined as the negative measure of tyranny — is the new definition of man in society and of man and society, freedom is self-regulation, self-regulation more difficult and more exacting than the intrigues of a tyrant. The demand for freedom, which turns against tyrants and parkways, against physical jerks and political economy, turns also against itself and nothing else; and so makes things very easy for tyrants.

A marathon runner is more free than a vagabond, and a cosmonaut than a sage in the state of levitation. Otherwise it would be more consistent to bark than write poems and to live in a leprosery than in San Francisco. Or Prague.

*

Certainly a poem is only a game.

Certainly a poem exists only at the moment of origin and at the moment of reading. And at best in the shadow-play of memory.

Certainly one can't enter the same poem twice.

Certainly a poet has the impression from the beginning that no purpose exists, as Henry Miller has said.

Certainly art becomes generally acceptable only when it declines into a mechanism and its order becomes a habit.

But in its aimlessness, in its desperate commitment to the word, in its primal order of birth and re-birth, a poem remains the most general guarantee that we can still do something, that we can still do something against emptiness, that we haven't given in but are giving ourselves *to* something.

The most general guarantee that we are not composed only of facts, of facts which, as Ernst Fischer says, are deeds withered into things.

Provided a poem, which is the poet's modest attempt to put off disintegration for a while, is not regarded as the philosopher's stone, bringing salvation and deliverance to stupefied mankind.

For art doesn't solve problems but only wears them
out.
For art is fidelity to failure.
For a poem is when nothing else remains.
Although . . .

IM/JM

Swans in Flight

It is like violence done to the atmosphere; as if Michel-
angelo reached out of stone. All the swans on the
continent take off simultaneously, interconnected by
a single circuit. They are circling around, which means
that Fortinbras' army is coming, that Hamlet will be
saved and the actors will play another act. In all trans-
lations, all theaters, behind all curtains, and without
mercy.

The actors are already growing wings against fate.

To hold on: that's everything.

DY/DH

Teaching About Diseases

Puppet diseases are tiny and thread-like, with funereal fur coats and huge ears. And little clawed feet.

There is no fever. Just sawdust sifting from the sleeves.

Diarrhea is like intellectual melancholy.

Irregular heartbeat is like the tick of deathwatch beetles.

It doesn't look like a disease, just attentive listening, which falls over the eyes like a hood.

When the strings break, that's the end. Just a carved chunk of wood on the bank of the river Lethe. And at the crossing, the little green man signalling: Walk!

Chin up, shouts the puppet-master. We'll play Macbeth. Everyone kicks the bucket in that play anyway. And the remaining puppets line up obediently backstage and pour out water from their little booties.

DY/DH

Brief Reflection on Cats Growing on Trees

Once upon a time, when moles still held their big
    conferences,
        and when they had better eyesight than they do
            now, the moles
        decided to find out just what was up there.

They elected a committee to supervise the project.
    This committee
        sent up a quick and clever mole who, when he
            left the motherland
        underground, spotted a bird sitting in a tree.

And so a theory was established; up there birds
    are growing on trees. But some moles
    considered this too simple. So they sent
    another mole up to learn more about birds
    growing on trees.

This time it was evening, and on the trees were
    squealing cats.
        Not birds, but squealing cats are growing on
            trees, announced
        this mole. An alternative cat-theory was there-
            fore established.

The two contradicting theories made it impossible
    for one neurotic
        member of the committee to fall asleep. He
            climbed up to see
        for himself. But it was night again, and pitch
            dark at that.

Nobody's right, announced the worthy mole.
  Birds and cats are
  optical illusions, which are evoked by the double
      refraction
  of light. Actually, he said, up there nothing is
      different
  from down here, only the earth is thinner and
      the roots on
  the other side are whispering something, but only
      a little, really quietly.

They approved this theory.

Since then, moles have stayed underground with-
  out establishing
  any committees, and they don't believe in cats,

or believe only a little.

SF/DH

Brief Reflection on Accuracy

Fish
   always accurately know where to move and when,
   and likewise
   birds have an accurate built-in time sense
   and orientation.

Humanity, however,
   lacking such instincts resorts to scientific
   research. Its nature is illustrated by the following
   occurrence.

A certain soldier
   had to fire a cannon at six o'clock sharp every
      evening.
   Being a soldier he did so. When his accuracy was
   investigated he explained:

I go by
   the absolutely accurate chronometer in the window
   of the clockmaker down in the city. Every day at five
   forty-five I set my watch by it and
   climb the hill where my cannon stands ready.
   At five fifty-nine precisely I step up to the cannon
   and at six o'clock sharp I fire.

And it was clear
   that this method of firing was absolutely accurate.
   All that was left was to check that chronometer. So
   the clockmaker down in the city was questioned
      about
   his instrument's accuracy.

Oh, said the clockmaker,
   this is one of the most accurate instruments ever.
      Just imagine,
   for many years now a cannon has been fired at six
      o'clock sharp.
   And every day I look at this chronometer
   and always it shows exactly six.

So much for accuracy.
  And fish move in the water, and from the skies
  comes a rushing of wings while

Chronometers tick and cannon boom.

EO

Brief Reflection on the Theory of Relativity

Albert Einstein, in conversation —
  (Knowledge is discovering
  what to say) — in conversation one day
  with Paul Valéry,
  was asked:

Mr. Einstein, how do you work
  with your ideas? Do you note them down
  the moment they strike you? Or only
  at night? Or the morning?

Albert Einstein replied:
  Monsieur Valéry, in our business
  ideas are so rare that
  if a man hits upon one
  he certainly won't forget it.

Not in a year.

EO

Brief Reflection on an Old Woman
with a Pushcart

Given: an old woman and a pushcart P.
Now you have a system of an old woman W and a
    pushcart P.

The system is moving from B the backyard to C the
    corner,
        from the corner C to R the rock, from the rock R
        to F the forest, from the forest F to H the horizon.

The horizon H is the point where vision ends and
    memory begins.

Nonetheless the system is moving
    at a constant rate V
    along a constant trajectory
    through a constant world and
    with a constant destiny
renewing its impulse and its sense from itself.

It's a relatively independent system;
in the regions from horizon to horizon
there's always one old woman with a pushcart.

So there's one geodesic unit once and for all.
    The unit of a journey there and back
    of autumn
    of our daily bread
    the unit of wind and low hanging sky
    of home in the distance
    of As we forgive others
    the unit of dusk
    of footprints and dust
    the unit of life's fulfillment amen.

SF/DH

Brief Reflection on Gargoyles

When the world was turning to stone
    cliffs grew out of diatoms, towns from sighs and
    imperatives from question marks.

When the world was turning to stone the angels living
    in mansard portals, behind cornices and
    steeples, stiffened into stale
    sulphuric devils. Gripping ledges with their
      tight claws
    they became gargoyles.

Now,
    they shoot off their mouths at passers-by,
    shouting:

    What are you staring at, you dodo!
    or:
    You are like dust, and to dust you shall return,
    or:
    Get otta here, stick to gravity!

When it rains, they pour out their hate in streams
    of water,
      shivering with delight and disrespect. At
        night they
      lick the ground with their pulpy tongues,
        making black
      white and vice versa.

As such, sometimes in spring, they're ashamed
    so they climb down, disguised as black cats
    and moonstruck marmots and fretfully criticize
    the gothic in general and gargoyles in particular
    Then curious angels without portfolio
    descend from their heights and listen,
    gripping the ledge with their claws.
    And so they harden, turning
    to sulphuric stone.

This insures
    the continuity of gargoyles,
    the consistency of gothic fonts
    and the respect of passers-by, cats and marmots
    for gravity.

SF/DH

Brief Reflection on the Butchering of Carp

You take a mallet
and a knife
and hit
the right spot so it doesn't flop because
flopping causes complications and lowers profit.

The people watching squint their eyes, admire
    your skill,
reach for their money. And the paper is ready
for wrapping. And smoke rises from chimneys.
Christmas gapes out from the windows, spreads
    along the ground
and splashes in vats.

Such is the Law of Happiness.

But I wonder, is the carp really the right animal?

Because a much better animal would be one
which — stretched out — kept flat — pinned down —
fixed its blue eye
on the mallet, the knife, the money, the paper
the people and chimneys
and Christmas.

And quickly
said something. For example

These are my best days, these are my golden days.
or
Starry skies above me and moral law in me.
or
And it *is* turning.

Or at least
Hallelujah!

SF/DH

Brief Reflection on Floods

We were brought up to believe
    a flood occurs when
    water rises above every limit,
    covers wood and dale, hill and mountain,
    places of temporary and permanent residence,

so that
    men, women, honored patriarchs,
    babes and sucklings, beasts of field and forest,
    creepycrawlies and heebee-jeebies
    huddle together on the last rocks
    sinking in the steely waves.

And only some kind of ark . . . and only
    some kind of Ararat . . . Who knows?
    Reports on the causes of floods vary
    strangely. History is a science
    founded on bad memory.

Floods of this nature should be taken lightly.

A real flood
    looks more like a puddle.
    Like a nearby swamp.
    Like a leaky washtub.
    Like silence.
    Like nothing.

A real flood is when bubbles
    come from the mouth
    and we think they're
    words.

SF/DH

Meeting Ezra Pound

I don't know what came first, poets or festivals.

Nevertheless, it was a festival that caused me to meet Ezra Pound.

They seated him in a chair on a square in Spoleto and pushed me towards him. He took the hand I extended and looked with those light blue eyes right through my head, way off into the distance. That was all. He didn't move after that. He didn't let go of my hand, he forgot the eyes. It was a lasting grip, like a gesture of a statue. His hand was icy and stony. It was impossible to get away.

I said something. The sparrows chirruped. A spider was crawling on the wall, tasting the stone with its forelegs. A spider understanding the language of a stone.

A freight train was passing through the tunnel of my head. A flagman in blue overalls waved gloomily from the last car.

It is interesting how long it takes for a freight train like that to pass by.

Then they parted us.

My hand was cold too, as if I'd touched the Milky Way.

So that a freight train without a schedule exists. So that a spider on a stone exists. So that a hand alone and a hand per se exists. So that a meeting without meeting exists and a person without a person. So that a tunnel exists — a whole network of tunnels, empty and dark, interconnecting the living matter which is called poetry at festivals.

So that I may have met Ezra Pound, only I sort of did not exist in that moment.   *SF/DH*

The Autumn Bus

Exhaling asthmatically, the front door opens. Tripping on the steps, passengers with turned-up collars rush in, burdened with bags and packages. Some hold gloves in their teeth. Others crush morning papers under their arms, feverishly searching themselves for change. Passenger Mrs. Nyklichek carries a child, which keeps sliding down. Passenger Holas waves his fist threateningly at the darkness outside.

The seated passengers, already in transit, watch with hostility.

Driver Chodura turns in disgust from the steering wheel to check the fares as they go into the cashbox. Numerous corrections and additions are required.

Chodura shuts the door, which closes with a screech. The lights are switched off.

The bus starts with a jerk. Passengers fumble around and stagger into its depths. The bus is underway.

Chodura turns to check the last fare.

CHODURA: (*huskily*) From the stunted coppice
     white steam is rising . . .
SEATED PASSENGERS: (*in chorus, with relief*)
     For fishermen, abandoned by water,
     For a black mirror with a tenfold image . . .
PASSENGER HOLAS: (*grabbing the overhead bar*)
     For empty veins of roads and ancient paving
       crews . . .
STANDING PASSENGERS: (*in chorus*)
     For girls guarding dead geese in grass,
     For foreign feathers in the fastidious fire . . .

Honking. The driver brakes. Passengers not holding bars lurch forward. Chodura spits through the half-opened window.

CHODURA: (*energetically*)
>Snow ripens in the fists of unborn babies . . .

SEATED PASSENGERS: (*getting up to exit*)
>And the spider in the eye sockets begins
>the story . . .

MRS. NYKLICHEK: (*pushing forward with the child, excitedly*)
>The tree of ice has sprouted and is broken by
>the sky . . .

PASSENGER HOLAS: (*at the door*)
>On this earth, we shall never meet again.

STANDING PASSENGERS: (*in chorus*)
>On this earth, we shall never meet again.

CHODURA: (*braking, switching the lights on*)
>On this earth . . .

SITTING PASSENGERS: (*in chorus*)
>. . . we shall never meet again.

The bus has stopped, the door has opened with a hiss. Suddenly, there is a deep, motionless silence.

CHILD OF MRS. NYKLICHEK:
>On this earth, we shall never meet again.

Far away, a honking is heard, but the silence persists. Nobody moves.

DY/DH

The Angel of Death

In an unspecified white hall, maybe the gym of a health resort or just Limbo, a line of corpulent citizens (C1 — Cn) seated on exercise bicycles pedal in pairs in a line from right to left. They wear white t-shirts and baggy, suspicious-looking sweatpants. They do not twitch, look up, turn around or otherwise distract themselves; they just pedal on as if the smooth running of the epoch depended on it.

A good-sized loudspeaker hangs above the row of cyclists, opening its black mouth and speaking in a sonorous, trustworthy voice.

LOUDSPEAKER: Citizens, such is the momentum of life. After the union of sexual cells, explosive reproduction and differentiation occur. The three embryonic layers give rise to tissues and organs and, you see, one begins breathing, digesting, kicking one's feet . . .

The citizens are pedalling more assiduously.

LOUDSPEAKER: . . . humoral factors and mediators are flowing out, thinking has begun, thoughts swim like glass fish in the black, prehistoric sea.

One citizen cleans his ear with his little finger; all keep pedalling.

LOUDSPEAKER: Self is distinguished from non-self. The frontiers of identity and the world are set. . . . The first cells mutate and degenerate, and the clock of life subtracts the first sum from the limited number of cell divisions. Birth takes place. One is leaving . . . for education courses, training, culture. One is exercising and economizing. The unmitigated enthusiasm circulates from capillaries to heart and back again, possibly through the lymphatic system too. One walks cheerfully down sad streets, and vice versa. One gambles in lotteries, and new horizons appear. Love is made. The increased level of sexual hormones ruins the thymus, control of malignant growth declines, malignancies occur, production of IgG antibodies declines, IgM antibodies cross-react with the tissues, rheumatism and diseases of collagen set in, atherosclerotic plates appear in coronary arteries, infarctions knock softly on the walls of the heart chambers . . .

The citizens, one after the other, start pedalling at a frenzied rate, struggling to ride away without leaving the spot.

LOUDSPEAKER: One walks sadly down sad streets, plaster falls. A balcony falls too. Maintenance has always been a problem.

Exhausted, the citizens return to their original speed, eventually wiping off the eventually heavy sweat.

LOUDSPEAKER: Freedom is the recognition of necessity. Here and there the number of cell divisions is exhausted. One is at one's wit's end. Jumping just in time from in front of buses. Buying lottery tickets. Creating values. Working after retirement. Culture is a function of working after retirement. One is turning into one's inward nature. The inward nature is the function of muscular atrophies. Blood circulation is often insufficient. Particularly in some places. Testosterone and a diet are introduced, and teeth are pulled out. It is the time of wisdom and merits.

The citizens pedal on and suffer.

LOUDSPEAKER: And then, citizens, then . . . comes the Angel of Death.

Darkness sets in. A blood-colored glow penetrates from the wings. Ponderous, fatal steps are heard, reminiscent of monotonous kettle drums. From the right enters — the Angel of Death. He is a small scrawny man in a rather shabby dark jacket and striped trousers worn at the knees. Has a forlorn briefcase and a bald head. He stops behind the last pair of cyclists at the right, so that none of the pedalling citizens can see him.

LOUDSPEAKER: An opportunity for you, citizens. A special compliment from the administration. This is your big chance. Speak to the Angel of Death. He stands behind you.

The citizens pedal on silently.

ANGEL OF DEATH: (*suddenly, like a sergeant*) Comrades, atten-shun! Pedal on, citizens, pedal! I'm telling it like it is: exercise, exercise, exercise! Because by exercising . . . You call that pedalling, Olejnik? . . . Olejnik, don't sit like a monkey on a melon . . . Because by exercising we strengthen our health. A solid health — hey, Opasek, pull up your pants, they're getting into your chain — a solid health, as well as walks outdoors in any kind of weather — Olejnik, stop staring and pedal — and a strong will prevents diseases. Prevention of diseases prolongs life. We live long — Opasek, put a new drawstring into that pair of pants, you'll never strengthen your health that way. We live long in order to . . . well, Olejnik? In order to . . .

The Angel of Death takes a cigarette out of his breast pocket and lights it. He blows the smoke at citizen Olejnik, pedalling in the pair in front of him.

Citizen Olejnik jumps down from his exercise machine, turns to the Angel of Death, and timidly stretches out his hand.

OLEJNIK: Olejnik, pleased to meet you, sir . . .
ANGEL OF DEATH: Karel Stac is my name.

They shake hands. Citizen Olejnik silently crumples and collapses. The Angel of Death puts his briefcase under his arm and climbs on the empty exercise bicycle.

ANGEL OF DEATH: (*triumphantly*) In order to exercise longer and better . . . We live longer in order to strengthen our hearts . . . We live longer in order to longer and better . . .

The Angel of Death moans the phrase rhythmically, and the citizens adjust their rate and pedal in time like marching soldiers, at attention and fully confident.

ANGEL OF DEATH: (*pedalling, speaking in a rhythmic chant*)
In order to longer and better . . .
In order to longer and better . . .

DY/DH

Crucifix

At the center of a huge table sits the Judge, in a very worn gown. On either side, the Assessors, made of cardboard. Below the table, right, a bench on which the little bird-like defendant huddles, flanked by beefy warders. Below the table, left, the Prosecutor, standing erect and mostly addressing the audience.

Above the Judge's head is a large crucifix, showing a Christ of athletic build, his loin cloth rather resembling Bermuda shorts. He puffs at a big cigar, held in his pierced and bleeding hand, now and then tapping ash in front of or on the Judge.

The proceedings are well under way.

PROSECUTOR: . . . of these repulsive crimes, yes crimes, what is especially significant, yes directly and enormously significant, is the pathological, though conscious, yes entirely conscious, even deliberately calculated and calculating affection for animals. Yes, animals.

The Defendant cringes even more.

PROSECUTOR: In his apartment he keeps — as has been testified to by witnesses and proven — he keeps, yes keeps, three cats, twenty-eight mice, five of them white, one iguana, and four, yes four, parakeets. He looks after them, feeds them, day and night. Yes, this . . . this . . . this individual, who has brought such affliction on his friends and neighbors, returns to his lair in order to let white and gray mice out of their cages and feed them on cheese, bacon, yes and bread and salt, in order to stroke, yes stroke with fingers soiled by so many machinations the warty skin of an iguana . . .

The Defendant, visibly shaken and head bowed, covers his face with his hands.

PROSECUTOR: . . . yes, an iguana, so that he could throw it drugged gnats, yes gnats, and give it infra-red ray treatment, so that he could fondle lazy and debauched cats and make them purr, yes purr, while . . .

The Prosecutor suddenly stops as if he has forgotten the text and lost the thread. He crouches apprehensively. At the same moment, the Defendant stands up straight. As if propelled by the same mechanism, Prosecutor and Defendant exchange places with a matter-of-course air of ritual. The Court and Warders do not move. The Defendant now stands in the Prosecutor's place, while the Prosecutor cringes between the Warders.

DEFENDANT: (*picking up the thread naturally, un-abashed*) . . . while his fellow-workers and comrades were groaning under the weight of the evil he had wrought. But he, cynically, yes, cynically . . .

The Defendant, drawing himself up to full height and pointing at the Prosecutor crouched between the warders, raises his voice with great feeling.

DEFENDANT: . . . was feeding his parakeets with what the mice had left, feeding them sunflower seed, yes seed, and stale rolls, yes, and even watched those gorged budgies preening themselves and billing and cooing. And this he did at a time when he was causing his neighbors, fellow-workers and comrades so much suffering . . . in the first place, because . . .
JUDGE: (*his concentrated attention distracted, booms out*) Please keep to the point!

The Prosecutor looks up for a moment, but the Defendant thunders on.

DEFENDANT: Yes, to the point. On the very day when so many mice had nothing to eat, when so many cats were whining helpless on the rooftops, when so many parakeets were threatened, yes threatened by polluted air and a shortage of sunflowers, on the very day when some iguanas, yes iguanas, were directly dying out, yes literally dying out, when, for example, only two specimens of the iguana *Ophisalis corneliana* were left alive and one didn't know where the other was . . . !

The Defendant breaks off and looks around in triumph. The Judge gazes idly at the clock.

JUDGE: (*raising his voice, almost hysterically*) Silence in the court! The hearing is adjourned. The Court will consult. Remain in your seats! The hearing will resume at ten o'clock.

The Judge gets up. He is not very tall and his gown trails after him oddly. The Warders also stand, stride in step to the Judge's chair, and grab him by the shoulders. Nonchalantly, they drag the feebly-wriggling judge out of the courtroom.

Prosecutor and Defendant go up to each other. One offers the other a cigarette. They light up and stand chatting.

Christ throws away his cigar and spits ceremoniously.

PROSECUTOR: You know, his nerves aren't what they used to be. In Disraeli's day, remember, we had trained crickets and eight squirrels —
DEFENDANT: Chickenfeed! Under Vespasian I tossed in a couple of young tigers.
CHRIST: (*uneasily*) Say, you guys, help me down, will you?
PROSECUTOR: What do *you* want? Just hang in there!

DY/DH

Sand Game

The corner of a park, lined with fragrant jasmine or mock-orange bushes (Philadelphus coronarius). *In the center a sandpit, all dug up, and behind it a smeared bench of unvarnished wood. Partly hidden by the jasmine, a woodshed, into which we can see through its pried-open door. Inside are shovels, hoes, wheel-barrows, and spilled bags of something or other.*

Seated on the bench is a relatively young white-haired grandpa, wearing a leather jacket and turtleneck sweater. He is reading a newspaper, which he holds open in front of him. Occasionally he peers over it.

In the sandpit, two relatively big children, Ilona and Robert, are playing. They have built a fairly complicated structure of sand, boards, wire and dog-shit. It reminds one of a rocket launching site or the gardens of Semiramis.

GRANDPA: (*peering over the newspaper*) They say it's going to be very windy and wet. So your fancy tricks'll be blown to kingdom come!

ROBERT: That's not really possible. An anticyclone is situated above Norway, but we are under the influence of very high barometric pressure, which is shifting slowly south.

GRANDPA: (*nettled*) But it's written here!

ILONA: The structure has an adequately firm foundation. We have considered all parameters. This flange here will withstand a pressure of 50 grams per square centimeter. The tolerances are considerable.

GRANDPA: (*more nettled*) You can't make something out of nothing. It doesn't matter a hoot to me what your to . . . tol . . . tolerances are. There's going to be a real gulley-washer. That's what they say here.

ROBERT: (*adding another little piece of wood*) The information flow is often burdened with considerable background noise. It is appropriate to relate the general and summary estimate to the concrete system which constitutes only a small segment of reality included with the information frame. In point of fact, the micro-climatic conditions of this sandpit can be defined only on the basis of physical evidence regarding all possible features of the regional formation.

ILONA: (*adding a sand patty*) Moreover, the essence of the artifact itself changes reality, or rather micro-reality, to the extent that the information preceding its creation cannot be fully valid, and therefore true, after it has been created.

ROBERT: The case is analogous to every anagenetic influence under natural conditions, which are never identical in relation to the new object nor to themselves, as soon as the object has passed from the sphere of intellectual conception to that of physical realization.

GRANDPA: You're crazy. Yesterday the sunset was blood-red and the birds were flying low. Here they say that a bridge collapsed in Ecuador. Wait a minute . . . not in Ecuador, in . . . what's it called, in Puerto Rico, no, in Malay — . . . in Malaysia . . . no, in Belgium.

ILONA: (*to Robert*) Here a few deep injections are needed.

ROBERT: (*to Ilona*) Certainly. Otherwise this extension would bring about such stress that, with the given material, we would exceed the original parameters.

GRANDPA: (*angrily*) You're crazy. He that mischief hatches, mischief catches. Nothing's going to change that, no matter how much you . . . you parameter yourself!

ROBERT: (*straightening up, though with the patience proper to his age*) In substantial thinking we can certainly relate the value of being, or even the value of its actual statement to a certain preformed model, in relation to which the being or statement appears one way or another insufficient, inadequate, or excessive. In such a case we can make use of verbal comparisons by means of which we release the dissatisfaction or frustration caused by the imminence of the preconceived model in our thinking, however we may look at it . . .

GRANDPA: Nutty as a fruitcake!

ILONA: But he is furthermore, and in my opinion right-ly, an adherent of non-substantial ontology . . .

ROBERT: (*beginning to walk about and expound in the manner of the Platonic school*) . . . for only in this way can we rise above the rigid structures of old or new anthropological reductionism and re-construct our world both in regard to its phenom-enology and to its freely and operatively substituted existentiality . . .

GRANDPA: (*waving his paper*) Oh, go to . . . Here they say . . .

ROBERT: (*with mounting enthusiasm, which results in the appearance of a small flickering and sparkling halo around his head, finally becoming a permanent green glow*) . . . to reconstruct the world in its meaningful comprehensiveness, and this, however, in awareness of our being within and consequently from the field we are trying to understand, but also to a certain degree on the basis of abstracting it from our own inness, on the basis of auto-objectivization and ad hoc derealization, which of course is in fact the beginning of real and lasting realization . . .

GRANDPA: You're crazy!

ROBERT: (*his head aglow with enthusiasm, enters the shed, stumbling over various kinds of mess, and is lost from sight*) . . . so that the reconstruction of the world in the system of non-substantial ontol-ogy . . .

From the shed comes an explosion, with pieces of fly-ing wood and clouds of dirty black smoke. Ilona sits down on the sand construction, squashing it. Grandpa jumps up, shielding his head with the newspaper. When the noise and smoke subside, a shaken Robert, now without his halo, creeps out of the shed.

GRANDPA: (*triumphantly*) Crazy as a loon!

DY/DH

Door II

Antechamber of an historical event. Heavy brocade curtains. In the middle a massive door leading into there. Above it, a coat of arms, ancient handiwork. In the corner, a solid table and chairs with pompous backs. In front, a pendulum clock, larger than life, ticking relentlessly. It strikes every two minutes, producing a dulcet sound.

Enter Fibbersoldier, investigates the room, listens at the curtain right, at the door, at the curtain left, circumspectly examines the pendulum clock and sets his own pocket pendulum clock accordingly. After which he circumspectly hides behind the pendulum clock.

Enter Captain (beard, pistol) and two soldiers (short swords and notebooks in hand).

CAPTAIN: Come here, Weissberger! Come here, Maximovitch!

Soldiers slouch around, shuffling in various directions, more away from than toward the Captain.

CAPTAIN: Well! The decisive moment is near. The greatest caution! caution! is imperative. Everything depends on the three of us! (*Louder*) We have to speak in a low voice. Are we alone?
SOLDIER WEISSBERGER: (*shouts*) We are!

The soldiers stop as far as possible from the Captain. Fibbersoldier lurks and listens. Now and then he writes a note on his cuff.

CAPTAIN: You, Weissberger, get ready at the door!

Weissberger sits comfortably at the table and throws his tools under the chair.

CAPTAIN: You, Maximovitch, will knock!

Maximovitch sits at the table and props his feet up.

CAPTAIN: (*with growing élan, moving down stage*)
You will enter and find out if he is asleep!
SOLDIER MAXIMOVITCH: (*behind the table, after a
long pause*) He's sleeping like a log.
CAPTAIN: Good! Find out if he's alone!
MAXIMOVITCH: (*behind the table, after a very long
pause*) He is.
CAPTAIN: This job is a piece of cake.

*He rubs his hands. He sits at the table and takes out a
flask, pours himself a gobletful, and drinks it. He offers
the flask to the soldiers, who gratefully but lazily take
swigs. Fibbersoldier creeps from his hiding place and
takes out a goblet, into which he slyly puts a few
drops of poison. He hands it to the Captain, who
pours. Fibbersoldier hurriedly drinks and hides.*

CAPTAIN: Draw!

Soldiers sit. Fibbersoldier lurks.

CAPTAIN: Jump and stab!

Soldiers sit.

CAPTAIN: (*with great enthusiasm*) History is . . . uh
what's . . . is watching you!

Soldiers sit.

CAPTAIN: (*excited, pours*) Stab above the fourth rib!
As we have taught you! Well! Above the fourth rib,
three fingers from the chestbone. Three fingers!

*Maximovitch drinks and raises his hand with three
fingers up. He scrutinizes his fingers with pleasure.*

CAPTAIN: And stab above the third rib too! One never
knows!

Soldiers sit and drink. Captain pours diligently.

CAPTAIN: Weissberger, follow Maximovitch!

Soldiers sit.

CAPTAIN: It isn't easy, but you'll make it!

Soldiers sit.

CAPTAIN: (*pours again*) Search the boxes! Take out
the papers! Don't step in anything!

Soldiers sit.

CAPTAIN: (*gulps down a gobletful*) Have you got it?

Soldiers sit and stare.

CAPTAIN: (*thrilled*) Have you got it?
WEISSBERGER: (*jerks, after a thoughtful deliberation*)
Yep.
CAPTAIN: Splendid! Excellent! The homeland will . . .
will . . . always remember you . . . or something.
Haven't you stepped in anything?

*Soldier W. falls asleep. Soldier M. slumbers, dreamily
caressing the leg of the chair with his finger.*

CAPTAIN: Cover all the traces! No one must find them.
Secrecy and super-secrecy! Stratagems and super-
stratagems!

*Fibbersoldier crawls from behind the clock, pours him-
self some poison, taps the Captain's shoulder and
hands him the goblet. Captain hurriedly pours.*

FIBBERSOLDIER: (*lugubriously*) Thanks.
CAPTAIN: You're welcome.

*Fibbersoldier hides again, drinking. Soldiers sit and
doze.*

CAPTAIN: And now, retreat! Weissberger to the right,
Maximovitch to the left! I will send a report to the

legate! Hurry! Eye for eye! Death for death! Measure for measure!

Everybody sits contently.

CAPTAIN: (*with maximum effort and enthusiasm*) Everything depends on accuracy. Everything depends on speed. The children will . . . will . . . learn about it . . . I think! Let us go! We are flying! We have won! For the legate! For the homeland! For lawfulness! For . . . (*he doesn't know, waves his hand*).

Everybody sits on. The clock strikes. All of a sudden the door creaks slightly and in the absolute silence begins to open; it is wide open and gapes. It leads into boundless darkness.

Fibbersoldier, lurking behind the clock, and the Captain notice it, watch with interest, but do not move. The soldiers sit and doze.

A soft, plaintive sound is suddenly heard from beyond the door; it gathers momentum, turning into tiny shrieks, barking, whining, lamenting and culminating in an inhuman, quivering howl.

DY/DH

Questioning

The greasy spoon Aurora. At the table moribund eaters and drinkers hunch over their plates, beer glasses and cups. At the hot food counter a solitary employee counts bills, which is obviously too much for him. There is an exit from the street, but no other door, because elderliness is not something anybody can pass through. Enter the middle-aged Questioner, dislocated in time and space. He hovers near the hot food counter for awhile, but fails to excite the counting employee's interest. Consequently, he turns to the table of Beer Drinkers.

QUESTIONER: (*timidly*) Excuse me please, can you tell me how to get to the pet store that sells birds?
FIRST BEER DRINKER: (*slightly intoxicated*) Whaddya need birds for, buddy?

In the ensuing silence only the scratching of cutlery in the gravy is heard.

SECOND BEER DRINKER: I knew a guy who had a cricket in a cage. It was some imported cricket.
FIRST BEER DRINKER: Did it make any noise?
SECOND BEER DRINKER: I guess it did. But in fact it was a stiff.
FIRST BEER DRINKER: Well, a cricket won't last, imported or not imported.
SECOND BEER DRINKER: A bird won't last either. I knew a guy . . .

The Questioner tries to attract attention.

SECOND BEER DRINKER: (*quickly*) . . . he used to buy stuff in that store. It's . . . it's round the corner . . . on the way to . . . what's its name . . . to Melnik.
FIRST BEER DRINKER: You crazy or something? It's round the third corner, like you go to the first traffic light and turn uphill, left, you see a sign saying Linen, but they sell surplus vegetables from co-ops, but most of the time the joint is closed.

SECOND BEER DRINKER: Well, you got it all wrong. For sure. It's round the corner, then you go down- hill, first uphill, see, and then down, that's the place where old Vokac slipped and fell on Abrham's car and Abrham was just starting the car and he got such a scare he backed the car up and knocked over that vegetable-seller's stand . . . but then he went forward and ran into that old bag's cart, the cart got going and they found it down at the reser- voir. . . . The vegetable guy ran out and cursed the broad, and she snapped at Abrham, and Abrham was so rattled he forget to step on the brakes and crashed into some garbage cans. Old Vokac was run over by somebody anyway, but no one knew if by Abrham or that cart or that guy who was driving by and stopped to help them. . . . Then they all put the blame on that old bag, but she wasn't in her right mind so they didn't get anything from her. So that's where it is, your store, where that cart passed.

The Questioner starts to retreat, but is stopped.

FIRST BEER DRINKER: You couldn't be more wrong, pal. That happened somewhere else, because Vokac went home from the On the Corner pub, and every- body in there heard it and went looking for that cart, because that woman had got lost. What pet store! That store is near the place where that blond broad used to live, that dame who had five kids and two daddies for each of them, ten altogether, so that each kid has a different family name, but also a different one from the daddies' names because they could never make up their mind about it, and she kept forgetting them. So the kids, they called each other by their family names, because all the boys were Peters and both girls were Marys. That blond dame could never think of any other name when she got knocked up. . . . So the kids used to hang around at the store window looking at them birds and monkeys, and they'd say, see Novak, I'd like that parrot, and Novak said, no way, Lederer, I want that monkey, right, Strniskova? So you see, it's round the third corner on the left, where that blond piece used to live.

During the discourse on the blond, eaters at the next table become interested, and an old woman with a tablespoon shuffles near from her finished soup.

SOUP WOMAN: Well, pardon me, I'm sure, but that blond dame lives at the water reservoir, where they had that fire so many times . . . and she's got eight kids and they (*flourishing her spoon like a rapier*) . . . they once almost burned down that green house, playing firemen, and that green house belonged to old Nemcova, she kept writing letters to her stepson in the army, he'd written her twice that he was killed in action, but he wasn't, he just wanted to get rid of her, but she just kept writing and only stopped when someone told her there was no war . . . so she started fixing up the place, thinking her son was coming back, and she put some old junk in the hall, and the blond dame's kids played there and almost set the house on fire, but the stuff didn't burn too well . . .

The Questioner makes an attempt to withdraw, but the Meat Eater approaching from the next table stops him.

MEAT EATER: (*clutching the Questioner's sleeve, as if intending to drag him to the witness box*) I don't know what you're talking about, but you could see that fire from as far as Vysocany, and it all happened two blocks from here. . . . And it was no kids who did it, it was spontaneous combustion. Spontaneous combustion is a special chemical process of unknown origin and I've found out . . .

Annoyance and grumbling flare up among the Beer Drinkers.

MEAT EATER: (*with increased effort*) . . . and it is provoked by the contact of two substances, for instance a hard and a soft substance, which makes the soft substance thicken and smolder, while the hard substance . . .

FIRST BEER DRINKER: Stuff it, where do ya get soft stuff in hay?

MEAT EATER: (*ignoring him*) . . . For instance, spontaneous combustion in writings bound in cloth or leather, while in stitched books . . .

SECOND BEER DRINKER: Yeah, but they gotta be rotten inside and you gotta have 'em near a stove.

MEAT EATER: Oh yes, I mean no, my *Health Guide* once caught fire and it spread to *The Classic Legends of Antiquity* . . .

The Beer Drinkers try to stop him and tug at the Questioner's clothes, as if it were all his fault, while the spoon-fencing Soup Woman grabs the floor:

SOUP WOMAN: You see, a fire, it's your destiny. If you are an Aries or a Cancer, and you got white spiders at home . . .

MEAT EATER: . . . and it also occurs when a dull and a smart material get in touch . . .

FIRST BEER DRINKER: Yeah, Abrham once went from the Bistro . . .

SOUP WOMAN: . . . and white spiders make white webs, and if they get into somebody's home, the person will die of fever or fire from those white webs . . .

MEAT EATER: . . . for instance, one Sunday afternoon, Stendahl . . .

FIRST BEER DRINKER: . . . and Vokac got run over for the second time . . .

SOUP WOMAN: . . . They don't see them white spiders and think they got black ones, but the fire is already on the roof . . .

SECOND BEER DRINKER: They got a fine mess at home!

MEAT EATER: . . . and therefore, he keeps his slim volumes of poetry . . .

They all flock together, shouting and waving their arms. The Questioner disappears in the sudden commotion.

SOUP WOMAN: (*shrieks*) . . . and those who have white webs in their hair . . .

FIRST BEER DRINKER: And Vokac got up and he says to the kid, Novak, where's that monkey . . .

SOUP WOMAN: . . . and whoever kills a white spider is sure to drown, like that old Nemcova, when she fixed up her place . . .

MEAT EATER: Because poetry also begins when dull and smart matters touch, tough and soft . . .

SECOND BEER DRINKER: And Vokac wrote on the wall: There's no Abrham//Abrham is gone!

SOUP WOMAN: . . . People don't know they have webs and no hair . . . But the webs keep catching and catching . . .

FIRST BEER DRINKER: Abrham said he couldn't run him over . . .

SOUP WOMAN: And the spiders were waiting and waiting . . .

Suddenly they all fall silent, because a skylark flies up above the counting employee, flutters below the ceiling, followed by their eyes, and sings as if a ploughman walked happily through his field. A cricket can be heard between the skylark's trilling notes. From the back emerges a king-size bird dressed in a hat and overcoat, and walks hesitantly among the tables.

FIRST BEER DRINKER: (*matter-of-factly*) Get a load of this! Must be some loony in that crazy outfit. What were we talking about?

DY/DH

Fairy Tales

A room in a cottage, cozy and warm. Real sweet home. In the corner, an old-fashioned stove. On the walls hang ancestral portraits, saints and statesmen, shelves with particularly big tins with spices, among which bay leaves look most prominent. There is no table. The stove faces a large window, strangely bare. Right under it is a stool with Granny on it, and other stools around with a finite number of children. Only the lamp at the stove is lit. It is almost dark, and the clear window seems to let in a strong night light.

GRANNY: (*with traditional kindness*) Once upon a time. In a green castle above the black forest lived a king and he had three daughters. But he was not a good king. He spoiled the ship for a ha'porth of tar, and there wasn't enough food to lure a mouse from a hole. The king was lantern-jawed, hatchet-faced and spindle-shanked. The princesses were always poorly. They had no servants and had to make two bites of a cherry left from breakfast last for lunch. Things went from bad to worse and they literally lived on air . . .

While Granny is speaking, a man in a leather coat and beret slowly emerges behind her back and presses his face against the window. The gleaming eyes stare inside, grow brighter, glow and glare. Hands with fingers spread touch the glass. When the figure has covered the whole window it suddenly disappears, probably stabbed or shot.

GRANNY: (*slightly halting*) . . . that they literally lived on air, so the king called his three daughters together and said . . .

An enormous rooster's head turns up behind the window, opening its beak. A clawed paw pushes forward and tears it down. Feathers swirl as if a flock of ravens has landed.

GRANNY: . . . and he said: Dear daughters, I don't

know what to do! I'll soon be pushing up daisies, and if this goes on, you won't get married till the cows come home. You have to wander in the world a bit. First . . .

Feathers swirl and a beautiful naked girl or something similar appears. She clutches at the window, but a bull's head rises behind her and black hairy hands seize her breasts and pull her down. A distant sound of broken glass is heard, long echoing in gusts of wind.

GRANNY: (*speaking louder*) First you, Annie. Take that dress out of the wardrobe, so you don't look like Job's turkey . . .

In a chaotic confusion, heads of cyclopes rush to the window, heads full of teeth, heads full of snakes, sticks full of eyes, trees full of legs, hands, hooves and stumps, and they soundlessly try to break in.

GRANNY: . . . go through the black forest . . .

Shadows of ghosts spill in, flutter through the room and cover everything.

GRANNY: . . . when you come to the village, knock at the door of the first cottage.

Like a shot, everything disappears, but the window and the wall split in the middle and frosty white light flows in. From the distance, two men in coats and berets approach with terrifying ease, spreading a black, growing cape. the cape covers more and more space with an impermeable black shade.

GRANNY: . . . when Johnny opens the door, tell him . . .

The music grows louder and fills the space. Then, in double-quick time, everything is as before. The window with the strong light, walls, the room, cozy and warm, portraits, tins with spices. Children on stools. But there is no Granny. Only the empty white stool. However, as before Granny's voice goes on:

VOICE FROM THE EMPTY STOOL: Once upon a time. In a green castle above the black forest lived a king and he had three daughters. But he was not a good king. He spoiled the ship for a ha'porth of tar, and there wasn't enough food to lure a mouse from a hole. The king was lantern-jawed, hatchet-faced and spindle-shanked.

One of the children, who have so far been quiet and immobile, turns to another.

CHILD: (*with a cheerful gesture*) I dig it, don't you?

DY/DH

How We Played the Gilgamesh Epic

Working mainly from the New Assyrian version, our puppet-master wrote a play unprecedented in the annals of puppet theater. Our troupe, he thought to himself, will be easy to cast for this:

Matysek the Gendarme will star as the mighty king Gilgamesh. He knows how to handle the drum and drumsticks, which he'll drop into limbo in Act Twelve. Enkidu, the hairy forest man, will be played by Beelzebub the devil; and the harlot, putting other thoughts into Enkidu's head, by the princess. Old Lady Skrhola will make a gorgeous Goddess Ishtar, she can strip a bit. Utnapishtim, who built the ark in the flood, will be impersonated by Gruntorad the Magician, without his hat of course! And we've got Franz the lackey and Rudolph the knight to take the parts of the gods Shamash and Enlil. But we have a problem with the monsters. The solution: Old Man Skrhola can be Humbaba the Giant, wearing the Dragon's head, and the rest of the Dragon can play the Heavenly Bull, since its leg can be easily unscrewed and hurled at Ishtar by Enkidu. Punch and Judy can change costumes as necessary to create extra goddesses, snakes, wolves, scorpions and the people of Ur.

In order to make the production okay for children, the puppet-master censored a few of the racy sequences, especially the fornication of Enkidu with the harlot, Gilgamesh's wedding with Ishtar and the edict against cohabitation in the city of Ur. This simplified the play considerably. The rest of the show was to be filled with hurdy-gurdy music, and the harlot would explain the advantages of a school education to Enkidu.

During rehearsals the puppet-master also decided to cut the fights and battles; their educational value was questionable, and the puppets were likely to break their strings. For example, in the fight between Gilgamesh and Enkidu, Beelzebub's nose was damaged, and Doctor Faustus, wearing Lucifer's hairy hide, had to stand in for him. So these scenes were replaced by lectures on geography by Michael the Water Sprite before the curtain.

Then it turned out that the sets
lacked a cedar forest, and that the roaring
of Humbaba the Giant gave the puppet-master
laryngitis. The swords with blades that weighed
two talents each and thirty-pound pommels and
    sheaths
got lost during rehearsals. The elamak-wood
    table,
the bowl of carnelian filled with honey,
and the bowl of lapis lazuli filled with butter
were never supplied.

To have the trap-door open
so that Enkidu's spirit could soar up
from the underworld, like a gust of wind,
was technically too difficult.
But everyone was hamming it up like hell:

Punch and Judy scamper in the square and yell:
    Oaruru, you created Gilgamesh,
    Now create his counterpart,
    Let him face his stormy heart,
    Let them meet and fight, and then
    Let Ur live in peace again.

Hairy Faustus sits in a meadow with the Princess,
    chanting:
    I will challenge him boldly,
    I will cry out in Ur:
    I am the strongest of all,
    I am the master of fate!
    I am he who was born in the hills,
    He who is mightiest.

Then the princess gives her passionate speech:
    Eat bread, Enkidu,
    It's the staff of life!
    And drink some beer, for such
    Is the custom of our country!

Matysek the Gendarme waves his halberd and
    howls from the ramparts:
        I want to help cut down the cedars!
        I want to win eternal glory!

Then Michael the Water Sprite lectures on
    forestry in Lebanon.
Skrhola enters, wearing the dragon's head:
        Let me go free, Gilgamesh,
        You'll be master, I'll be servant.
        The trees I've grown I'll fell for you,
        And houses I shall build for you.

As soon as Skrhola drops dead, discreetly,
his missus under the lime tree cries:
        If you don't make the Bull of Heaven for me,
        I'll shatter the gates of the underworld,
        I'll uproot the gate-posts,
        I'll summon the dead to devour the living . . .

Faustus promptly throws the dragon's leg at her,
and Franz the lackey plays it very annoyed.

And the puppet-master,
buoyed up by all the action,
keeps telling the puppets what a hit this epic is,
and rushes them round the stage,
jerking their hands and feet at random,
and even recites the connecting texts
in a robust contrabass,
and in the verbal flood
Sumerian remnants paddle around
while the puppet-master bawls:
        Who's the most beautiful hero
        Who's the greatest of men?
and he kicks the spotlight of Shamash the God
while verses are heard through the chaos:
        Along the road of the sun he went.
        One double-hour he traveled;
        Dense is the darkness and there is no light.
        He can see neither before nor behind.
        Four double-hours he traveled;

Dense is the darkness and there is no light.
He can see neither before nor behind.
Six double-hours he traveled;
Dense is the darkness and there is no light.
He can see neither before nor behind.
Eight double-hours he traveled, crying out:
Dense is the darkness and there is no light.
Nine double-hours, the north wind in his face.
He can see neither before nor behind . . .

and nobody knows who is who,
the curtain is torn and so is the cap
of Punch, the friend of children,
and everyone goes home, not knowing where,
and Michael the Water Sprite
before the curtain, still on stage
unharmed by the stampede
quietly quotes Enkidu —
Heaven was calling, Earth answered.
And I stood all alone.

and adds, Gee, that's a knockout,
an epic like that.
And anyway, we'll never
get parts like that again.
Never.

DY/DH

Scene with Fiddlers

It snowed from the heart. And for years.

On we went, the clarinet an icicle,
the fiddle shivering under the coat. It was getting dark
in a gaping landscape. Beyond the hill
some pig, in mortal agony. No trace of music,
only silence, thickening.

All our life
we've been struggling through snowdrifts,
from portal to portal, from left to right.

And at the very end,
breathless, thoughtless, and therefore
weightless, in all that silence
somebody tootled.

Toot, an ember of music. Toot,
music itself.

So that the road, the snow,
the scene and the silence
could be
subtracted from eternity.*

DY/DH

*Jaroslav Seifert

Punch's Dream

I'll come out before the curtain, trying hard
not to tangle my strings
among the sets.
I'll jingle my bells,
whip off my cap,
and before the puppet-master can collect his wits,
I'll speak in my own voice,
you know,
my own voice,
my own thoughts,
for the first and last time,
because then they'll put me back in the box
and wrap me in tissue paper.
I'll say what I've felt
all through the ages of wood.
I'll say, no matter how silly my tiny voice
sounds, how embarrassingly squeaky,
I'll say the most serious and crucial thing,
I'll speak my piece . . .

I hope they'll hear me.
I hope they'll understand.
I hope they won't laugh.
I hope it grows in the children
and pricks the grownups.
I hope it changes the color of the sets.
I hope it agitates the cardboard
and the spotlight-shadows. I hope it alters
the law of relativity.
I'll say . . . Hello, hello, hello,
And welcome to our show!

DY/DH

The Sorcerer's Lament

At first it was too wet.
          So one did not practice magic.
Then the fountains dried up, the yeast
miscarried, water snakes
became watch-chains and
watercolors turned into
the sand of heavenly roads.
          So that it was impossible
          to practice magic.

For a couple of years I was busy
filling out white mouse taxation forms.
The King had a lasting controversy
with the Queen, wallpaper grew ears,
flames rolled up like sheets of linoleum,
and thunder struck the harpsichord.
          So that one could not recognize
          whether one was practicing magic
          or not.

Finally, there was a total shortage
of bats. I made them out of paper,
but they looked more like little flying pigs.
And they were chewed up by thready hookworms
of the typewriter strain. The magic wand
got pregnant by a retired saint.
My apprentices took to the bottle.
          In fact, I sort of never started
          practicing magic.

But my great magic is that I'm
still here. With a medium-sized
halo around both heads.

DY/DH

Ganesha

Siva the god was such a hothead.

When his little son bugged him in the bath,
he chopped his head off. Then
he had second thoughts, the way
metaphysicals usually do,
and provided his son, Ganesha,
with the head of a baby elephant,
executed *ad hoc.*

So that Ganesha was the first transplant patient.
So that the rest of the elephant
vanished from history.

So that Ganesha made a nice living
as a monster. He rides on a rat
and visits us at Christmas,
asking what kind of Siva
has chopped off
our head
this year.

DY/MH

4
(pathology)

Reality

The small worms of pain still wriggled
   in the limpid air,
The trembling died away and
Something in us bowed low before
   the fact of the operating-table
   the fact of the window
   the fact of space
   the fact of steel
   with seven blades.

The silence was inviolable
   like the surface of a mirror.

Though we wanted to ask
Where the blood was flowing
And
Whether you were still dead,
   darling.

GT

Suffering

Ugly creatures, ugly grunting creatures,
Completely concealed under the point of the needle,
   behind the curve of the Research Task Graph,
Disgusting creatures with foam at the mouth,
   with bristles on their bottoms,
One after the other
They close their pink mouths
They open their pink mouths
They grow pale
Flutter their legs
   as if they were running a very
   long distance,

They close ugly blue eyes,
They open ugly blue eyes
   and
   they're
   dead.

But I ask no questions,
no one asks any questions.

And after their death we let the ugly creatures
   run in pieces along the white expanse
   of the paper electrophore
We let them graze in the greenish-blue pool
   of the chromatogram
And in pieces we drive them for a dip
   in alcohol
   and xylol
And the immense eye of the ugly animal god
   watches their every move
   through the tube of the microscope

And the bits of animals are satisfied
like flowers in a flower-pot
   like kittens at the bottom of a pond
   like cells before conception.
But I ask no questions,
   no one asks any questions,
Naturally no one asks
Whether these creatures wouldn't have preferred
   to live all in one piece,
   their disgusting life
   in bogs
   and canals,
Whether they wouldn't have preferred to eat
   one another alive,
Whether they wouldn't have preferred to make love
   in between horror and hunger,
Whether they wouldn't have preferred to use
   all their eyes and pores to perceive
   their muddy stinking little world
Incredibly terrified,
Incredibly happy
In the way of matter which can do no more.

But I ask no questions,
   no one asks any questions,
Because it's all quite useless,
Experiments succeed and experiments fail,
Like everything else in this world,
   in which the truth advances
   like some splendid silver bulldozer
   in the tumbling darkness,

Like everything else in this world,
   in which I met a lonely girl
   inside a shop selling bridal veils,
In which I met a general covered
   with oak leaves,

In which I met ambulance men who could find no
    wounded,
In which I met a man who had lost
    his name,
In which I met a glorious and famous, bronze,
    incredibly terrified rat,
In which I met people who wanted to lay down
    their lives and people who wanted to lay down
    their heads in sorrow,
In which, come to think of it, I keep meeting my
    own self at every step.

GT

In the Microscope

Here too are dreaming landscapes,
lunar, derelict.
Here too are the masses
tillers of the soil.
And cells, fighters
who lay down their lives
for a song.

Here too are cemeteries,
fame and snow.
And I hear murmuring,
the revolt of immense estates.

GT

Pathology

Here in the Lord's bosom rest
the tongues of beggars,
the lungs of generals,
the eyes of informers,
the skins of martyrs,

in the absolute
of the microscope's lenses.

I leaf through Old Testament slices of liver,
in the white monuments of brain I read
the hieroglyphs
of decay.

Behold, Christians,
Heaven, Hell, and Paradise
in bottles.
And no wailing,
not even a sigh.
Only the dust moans.
Dumb is history
strained
through capillaries.

Equality dumb. Fraternity dumb.

And out of the tricolours of mortal suffering
we day after day
pull
threads of wisdom.

GT

The Bomb

Murder in the lithosphere.
Clay burst from the rock,
fire flowed from the clay.

At the base of the crater
a naked, tender, loving
frog's heart
still beats.

DY/MH

Explosion

Yes;
but then came
bricklayers,
doctors,
carpenters,
    people with shovels,
    people with hopes,
    people with rags,
stroked
the loins of the wild house,
stroked
the pounding heart of space,
stroked the crest of pain

until all the bricks came back,
until all the drops of blood came back,
all the molecules of oxygen

and stone
pardoned stone.

IM/JM

The Dead

After the third operation, his heart
pierced like an old carnival target,
he woke in his bed and said:
Now I'll be fine,
like a sunflower. And have you ever
seen horses make love?

He died that night.

And another one plodded on for eight
milk-and-water years
like a long-haired water plant
in a sour creek,
as if he stuck his pale face out
on a skewer from behind
the graveyard wall.

Finally the face disappeared.

In both cases the angel of death
stamped his hobnailed boot
on their medulla oblongata.

I know they died the same death.
But I don't believe they're dead
in the same way.

DY/DH

Collision

I could have been dead by now,
he said to himself, ashamed, as if
it was the heart's malediction, lifting a bundle of bones
to a man's height, as if it was
a sudden restriction from even touching the words —
Danger / High Voltage.
Anyway, he was afraid to find
his own body pressed in that metal. Painful —
down to the capillaries.

The streetcar stood jammed over him
like an icebreaker's bow; what was left
of the car was a funny pretzel
bitten by the dentures of a mad angel.
Something dark was dripping onto the rails,
and a surprisingly pale wind
leafed through the pages of a book
that was still warm.

People formed in a ring and with deaf-mute
sympathy waited for the play's
catharsis, like black mites
creeping from under the wings
of a freshly-beheaded hen.
A distant siren's wail moved closer,
turning solid in the hexed air-conditioning
of that day and that minute.
Dewdrops fell on the back of the neck,
like remnants of atmospheric dignity.
Painful, down to the capillaries.

No thanks, he said, I'll wait;
because a silent film had begun to run,
without subtitles, without colors,
without answers.

        And what about magnetic monopoles
fleeing seconds after the Big Bang,
protons violating the principle
of time reversal variance.

The giant molecular cloud complexes
delivering embryonic stars.

The loneliness of the first genes
accumulating amino acids
in shallow primeval puddles,
on the collateral of entropic loan sharks.

Dried starfish
like hawk's talons, grasping the bottoms
of vanishing seas.

Mortal migrations of birds
obeying the sun's inclination
and the roar of sexual hormones.

The caged, half-crazed
orangutan who vomits to pass the time.

Mice that learned to sing
and frogs, balancing on one foot like the thigh
of a Mesopotamian beauty queen.

Poetry, an occupation
so messy it makes the slide-rule bend,
and supervisors increasingly cross-eyed.

What about the girl in the leukemia ward
on the toilet, wanting to show
what a mustache the good doctor has —
when she gestures with her skinny sticks of hands
she starts to slide through the seat, grabs it,
gestures, grabs, again and again.

And what about the lousy egghead,
the associate professor who almost
understood the approximate universe
and forgot about the traffic rules?

No thanks, he said to some uniform,
I don't need anything. I have my license
in my pocket, but I can't reach it.
And he tried to smile a little
about this painfully embarrassing,

finished creation.
It's all my fault, he said,
thank you.

And then he died.

DY/DH

Brief Reflection on the Word 'Pain'

Wittgenstein says: the words 'It hurts' have replaced
    tears and cries of pain. The word 'Pain'
    does not describe the expression of pain but
        replaces it.
    Thus it creates a new behaviour pattern
    in the case of pain.

The word enters between us and the pain
    like a pretence of silence.
    It is a silencing. It is a needle
    unpicking the stitch
    between blood and clay.

The word is the first small step
    to freedom
    from oneself.

In case others
    are present.

EO

Distant Howling

In Alsace,
on July 6, 1885,
a rabid dog knocked Joseph Meister down
and bit him fourteen times.

Meister was the first patient
saved by Pasteur's
vaccine, in thirteen
gradually increased doses
of weakened virus.

Pasteur died of ictus
ten years later.
Fifty years later
the watchman Meister

committed suicide
when the Germans
occupied Pasteur's institute
including the poor dogs.

Only the virus
never got involved.

DY/DH

Interferon

Always just one demon in the attic.
Always just one death in the village. And dogs
howl in that direction, while from the other way
the newborn child comes, just one,
to fill the empty space in the big air.

Likewise, cells infected by a virus
send signals out, defenses
are mobilized, and no other virus
gets a chance to settle down
and change the destiny. This phenomenon
is called interference.

And when a poet dies, deep in the night,
a lone black bird wakes up in the thicket
and sings for all it's worth,
while a black rain trickles down
like sperm or something,
the song is bloodstained, the suffocating bird
sings perched on an empty thorax
where the imaginary heart
wakes up to face its forever interfering
futility. And in the morning, the sky's swept clean,
the bird's sleepy, the soil's fertilized,
and the poet is gone.

In Klatovska Street, in Pilsen,
by the railway bridge, there was
a small shop that sold quilts and comforters.
In times when what is needed
is a steel cover for the whole continent,
the quilt business is slack.
The shopkeeper was in trouble.
In such times men of the world
usually turn to art.

In the big shop window
the shopkeeper built
a cottage of quilts and comforters
and staged a performance every night
about a quilted cake-house and a red-quilted

Little Red Riding Hood, while his wife,
in this stuffed masquerade,
played the wolf or the witch,
and he was the padded Hansel,
Gretel, Red Riding Hood or Granny.
To see the two old people
crawling in monstrous floods of textile
around the plump cottage
was not unambiguous.

It was something like the life
of sea cucumbers in the mud
under a cliff. Outside
the surf of war roared and they
carried on their puffy
pantomime, out of time and out of action.

Children used to watch from the street
and then go home. Nothing was sold,
but it was the only pantomime around.

The black bird sang
and the rain poured into the thorax
marked with the Star of David.

But in the actors under the quilts,
l'anima allegra must have woken up
at that moment, so that,
sweating and rapt, they played
the undersea *commedia dell'arte*
thinking there was no backstage
until a scene was over, moving jerkily
from shopwindow to cottage and back,
with the gaiety of polio-stricken Columbines,
while the sound of drums and bugles never
        reached them.

Or else they thought such a deep
humiliation of old age
and its traditional dignity
interfered with the steps
of men in leather coats
and departures of trains

for human slaughterhouses.
It did.

The black bird sang
and the ravaged sclerotic hearts
hopped in their chests,
and then one morning they did not play,
did not raise the shutters,
the sky was swept clean, the soil fertilized,
the comforters confiscated for the eastern front
and the actors transferred to
the backstage of the world
called Bergen-Belsen.
In place of the quilt shop now
a greengrocer peddles rubbery kohlrabies.

Always just one death in the village.
Always just one demon.
How great is the power of the theater, even if
it ends up collapsing
and vanishing backstage.

Dogs howl in that direction.
And the butterfly pursues
those who stole the flowers.

When we did autopsies
at the psychiatric ward in Bohnice,
in air thick with the urban pollution
of relative futility,
the car would pull up before the barracks
and the inmates would wave
some sort of Labor Day parade flags
from the windows
as one went, hugely alone,
to the solitary mortuary
beyond a grove of trees
where the naked bodies
of ancient schizophrenics
waited, along with two live inmates,
one pulling the corpses up from the basement
on a dumbwaiter and putting them gently
on tables, as a mother would

her unbaptized child,
the other lurking in a dark corner
with a pen dipped in ink
to write the Latin protocol,
his spelling faultless,
and nobody uttering a sound, only
the moan of the elevator shaft . . . and the knife
slicing the epidermis and dermis made
a sound like tearing silk . . . and it was always
powerful and unprecedented pneumonias
and tumors big as dragon's eggs,
the rain soaked the thorax
and in the roaring silence
one had to break the line of an angel's fall
and dictate the logical sentence
for the ghoul, doomed ages ago . . .
and the schizophrenic's pen in the corner
diligently scratched the paper
like an eager mouse.

We need no prompter,
the puppets said proudly.

The air of this anatomic theater
was filled with interferon,
it was a spectacular personal charge
against the malignant growth, it was
a general amnesty of walls, entropy
was forsworn for the moment,

because there are no bubbles at the bottom
to be cracked by the breeze.

The red balloon outside
soared to the unseen heaven, its chains
stretched by knowing
the nearer the inferno
the greater the paradise,
the nearer the prison cell
the greater the freedom.

Cantabit coram latrone omne vacuus viator.

And that is the fierce essence of the theater,
when the actor stripped of everything
rises to the top of the conflagration
and everything else is hushed
like a much-hunted animal
with muscles still trembling
but with endorphines
and an immense peace in the brain.

Yes, even a whale will sometimes leave the herd
to hurl itself into shallow water and die in the sun
like a collapsed cathedral, with a pushed-out penis,
and death is buried instantly
in a tiny grain of sand
and the sea is laughing.

Ask felled trees; in broken speech
they preach about saplings. In the galactic
jargon of white dwarves
stars of the main sequence
shine forever.

In the non-Euclidean curved space
which passes comprehension as
the interference of the theater does,
you hear forever the voices of children
from the elementary school of death,
children from kitchen puppet tragedies,
and children from military junkets
when spearing and subsequent flinging of legs
was something like curry,
the condiment of mercenary marches,
voices of children passing comprehension —

But we washed behind our ears,
we didn't pull the cat's tail,
we haven't put
our fingers into sockets —

What else is left
in the universe of hominization
slow as the decay of tritium,

except learning about the growing shame of
        demons —
since the time of the Aztecs, high priests
haven't presented offerings while dressed
in the skin of a freshly skinned prisoner.

We need no prompter, said —

One Christmas, a drunk
dressed up as a devil
fell down the stairs and lay there,
and a child, experiencing
that embarrassing joy just inches from fright,
ran out, upon hearing the noise, and called —

Mummy, come here, there's a dead devil —

And he was, although the actor got up
after another sip. Maybe dogs howled,
but only by a dark mistake.
The stars of the main sequence shone,
the bird was about to sing in the saplings,
the child trembled a little
from the chill of three million years,
in the big air, and was told,
poetically,

it's all just a game,
look, the butterfly's bringing
the flowers back . . . and
there's no other devil . . . and
the nearer the paradise . . .

It believed and it didn't —

                                    DY/DH

While Fleeing

It was Rembrandt
or Poincare,
or Einstein,
or Khatchaturian,
two years old,
and his mother
was shot
or buried
in rubble
while fleeing
and she was pressing him
to her breast
when she fell,
he was smothered,
and disappeared without having appeared.

When we find
small white stones
or a yellow pebble,
we play with them,
we put them together
in little piles,
letters,
and circles.

It may be an
unconscious
burial rite
for times when
there aren't any
passage graves,
cremation sites,
bronze clasps

when only
a couple of million
mothers flee
constantly flee
from somewhere to
somewhere
else.   *DY/DH*

The Earth is Shrinking

The earth is shrinking,
there's
almost no place to set a flowerpot.
And rain-worms get confused
and intertwine
in knots
like fibrilatory tangles
in the brain
of a slightly crazy
temple dancer.

The earth is shrinking.
Maybe
due to the evaporation
of good intentions.
Maybe
due to the lifting
of a baldachine
over the head
of a saintly
marsupial.

Certainly
due to the dead
devouring the earth.
For a hundred thousand years
the dead have been settled in,
packed down, eating earth

excreting marsupial
good intentions.

DY/MH

Spinal Cord

Solomon's flute in elastic ivory,
the organ pipes
of the white Aurora Borealis,
the singing of dolphins and sirens,
crest of a blind
cave
fish.

Braided white
Christmas loaf of nerves,
irregular Latin verbs
in place of mystery.

The computer's anthology of tenderness
in Pascal.

Enclosed, as always,
in the black rings
of a vertebra,
    a vertebra,
     a vertebra,

because otherwise,
immaculate or not,
we'd all be paralyzed
right after birth.

DY/DH

Heart Failure

The airport is closed.
The plane circles round like
a fixed idea
over the closed city,
over porters, over dogs,
over troughs, over not-for-sale window-dressing,
over mailmen, roosters, and hens,
over brewers and tiny springs.
The airport is closed.

> Tiny Spring, give water
> to my little Rooster:
> He's lying in the yard
> with his feet up —
> I'm scared he'll die.

Water dripping from faucets,
the city tumbling down.
There are no matches
for the synthesis of a star.
Somebody has stolen Charon's paddle,
it's strictly forbidden to use the ferry,
the Last Judgment's postponed,
come next week,
spring will be pink
as Aphrodite's ass.
Water dripping from faucets.

> Miss Seamstress, give a scarf
> to the tiny Spring, it will
> give water to my little Rooster:
> He's lying in the yard
> with his feet up —
> I'm scared he'll die.

The museum is bulging.
Tiny letters crawl out
like water fleas,
and even the trees scratch themselves.
Drowned dictionaries float.

On top a golden inscription
— Curse Those Who Hate Art —
Down below, the split, tinkered-up
museum is bulging.

Mister Shoemaker, give shoes
to Miss Seamstress,
Seamstress will give a scarf to tiny Spring,
tiny Spring will give water
to my little Rooster:
He's lying in the yard
with his feet up —
I'm scared he'll die.

Tender madness of ashes
in the lungs of the streets.
Black blood of poetry
in the veins of the pavement.
Street cleaners fall behind in their work.
In the madding crowd
somebody knelt down;
So what, they say,
so what, and they're right.
Tender madness of ashes.

Good Swine, give your bristles
to Mister Shoemaker,
Shoemaker will give shoes to Seamstress,
Seamstress will give a scarf to tiny Spring,
tiny Spring will give water
to my little Rooster:
He's lying in the yard
with his feet up —
I'm scared he'll die.

To bear at least one destiny, darling.
You are here but at the same time
you're crying far away.
Home is like a closed
metal rose and dead loves
knock on the roof with little parched fists.

And the one and only tear circles round
as the thirteenth planet,
transparent, uninhabited,
absolutely useless.
To bear at least one destiny.

Mister Brewer, give the Swine some draff,
Swine will give her bristle to Shoemaker,
Shoemaker will give shoes to Seamstress,
Seamstress will give a scarf to the tiny Spring,
Spring will give water to —

— Damn it, I can't remember to what . . .
The empty barrels of heaven rumble
right over our heads,
at night deep down inside
lions roar in thimbles,

And in the cracking of vertebrae
and the yelling of arteries
somebody is singing

— tiny Spring, give water,
in the yard, in the yard,
in the yard, in the yard,

somebody is singing on and on
just like that —

Probably the little rooster.

SF/DH

Pompeii

In Pompeii
on the clattering paved
Venus Road
in full ancient sun
Little Red Riding Hood
drags her gift basket.

Such a beautiful moment.

Granny has
genital herpes, but
she doesn't know what that is.

Cholera is baked
in the pie.
But centurions
don't believe in infections.

Such beautiful times.

In the distance
Mt. Vesuvius groans and gas
burns,
but geology
ended with Empedocles
in the mouth of Mt. Etna.

Such a perfect epoch.

The glow-worm 'gins to pale his uneffectual fire.
Soon
everyone will be baked
in the stony mud
like raisins of immortality,

and during excavations echoes will resound
of wolf chorales, Hamlet chorales, concubine chorales
about the good old times.

DY/DH

Kuru, or the Smiling Death Syndrome

We aren't the Fores of New Guinea,
we don't indulge in ritual cannibalism,
we don't harbor the slow virus that
causes degeneration
of the brain and spinal cord with spasms, shivers,
progressive dementia and
the typical grimace.

We just smile,
embarrassed, we smile,
embarrassed, we smile,
embarrassed, we smile.

DY/DH

Vanishing Lung Syndrome*

Once in a while somebody fights for breath.
He stops, getting in everyone's way.
The crowd flows around, muttering
about the flow of crowds,
but he just fights for breath.

Inside there may be growing
a sea monster within a sea monster,
a black, talking bird,
a raven Nevermore that
can't find a bust of Athena
to perch on and so just grows
like a bullous emphysema with cyst development,
fibrous masses and lung hypertension.

Inside there may be growing
a huge muteness of fairy tales,
the wood-block baby that gobbles up everything,
father, mother, flock of sheep,
dead-end road among fields,
screeching wagon and horse,
I've eaten them all and now I'll eat you,
while scintigraphy shows
a disappearance of perfusion, and angiography
shows remnants of arterial branches
without the capillary phase.

Inside there may be growing
an abandoned room,
bare walls, pale squares where pictures hung,
a disconnected phone,
feathers settling on the floor
the Encyclopedists have moved out and
Dostoevsky never found the place,

lost in the landscape
where only surgeons
write poems.

DY/DH

*Burke.

173

Crush Syndrome*

Once when, in winter dark,
I was cleaning the concrete-mixer,
its cogwheels, like the teeth
of a bored rat of Ibadan,
snapped up the glove
with the hand inside. The finger bones
said a few things you don't hear very often
and then it grew quiet, because
even the rat had panicked.

In that moment
I realized I had a soul.
It was soft, with red stripes,
and it wanted to be wrapped in gauze.

I put it beside me on the seat
and steered with the healthy hand. At the clinic,
during the injections of local anesthetic
and the stitching,
the soul held firmly with its mandibles
to the stainless-steel knob of the adjustable table.
It was now whitish crystal
and had a grasshopper's head.

The fingers healed.
The soul turned, at first,
to granulation tissue,
and later a scar, scarcely visible.

DY/DH

*Bywaters.

174

Anencephaly

(Newborn without a brain)

And Jonah was in the belly of the fish
three days and three nights.
And what kind of Jonah?

This one reclines in a crib on the ward,
has the face of a pink toad
and instead of a skull
                a bag,
                        a limp red bag,
pulsating on the pillow.

His mouth-opening forms at times
a short proboscis
like a tapir searching in bamboo
for Saint Anthony.

And Erato the muse howls with sorrow in the elevator.

But he is brotherly, he is close
to Nature,
            to cauliflower,
                        to porcupines,
he is genuine, more genuine
than Broca's brain and Kant's reason,

he is innocent, more innocent
than Noah's offspring in the land of Shinar,
than original sin,
than Lucifer's mafia,
than the thief on the right-hand cross,

Bergson's seventh reincarnation,
or a surrealist's daydream.
And what kind of surrealist?

He drinks and excretes,
as decreed by the laws of Mother Earth.

Only a couple
                    of tainted genes too many
only a couple
                    of vile enzymes behind the poem,

a tiny avant-garde miracle.
And *who would first cast a stone?*

Perhaps he has *opened the seventh seal*
and there is *silence in heaven*
about the space of half an hour, and *the seventh angel*
poured out his vial into the air,
and there came a great voice
out of the temple of heaven, saying,
                                        It is done.

                                        DY/MH

Intensive Care Unit

God's insects stuck on pins
betrayed heroes of the abdominal cavity.

Cracked faience of whining puppets,
human soul dripping from plastic tubes.
Behind white curtains a scene
from the war of the salamanders
is endlessly getting ready.

And liturgies change
and souls change
and blushings and palenesses change
and winged prophets change
and writers of chronicles change and
gods change.

But amikacin,
the antibiotic,
is the only one.

DY/DH

Heart Transplant

After an hour

there's an abyss in the chest
created by the missing heart
like a model landscape
where humans have grown extinct.

The drums of extracorporeal circulation
introduce
an inaudible
New World Symphony.

It's like falling from an airplane, the air growing
    cooler and cooler,
until it condenses in the inevitable moonlight,
the clouds coming closer, below the left foot, below
    the right foot,
a microscopic landscape with roads like capillaries
pulsing in counter-movements,
feeble hands grasping for the King of Blood,
"Seek the Lord while he may be found,"
ears ringing with the whistles of some kind of cosmic
    marmots,
an indifferent bat's membrane spreading between the
    nerves,
"It is unworthy of great hearts to broadcast their own
    confusion."

It's like falling from an airplane
before the masked face of a creator
who's dressed in a scrub suit
and latex gloves.

Now they are bringing, bedded in melting ice,
the new heart,
like some trophy
from the Eightieth Olympiad of Calamities.

Atrium is sewn to atrium,
aorta to aorta,
three hours of eternity
coming and going.

And when the heart begins to beat
and the curves jump
like synthetic sheep
on the green screen,
it's like a model of a battlefield
where Life and Spirit
have been fighting

and both have won.

DY/DH

5

(tautology)

What Else

What else to do
but drive a small dog
out of yourself
with a stick?

Scruff bristling with fright
he huddles against the wall,
crawls in the domestic zodiac,
limps,
bleeding from the muzzle.

He would eat out of your hand
but that's no use.

What else
is poetry
but killing that small dog
in yourself?

And all around the barking, barking,
the hysterical barking
of cats.

DY/DH

The Best Room, or Interpretation of a Poem

And now tell it to me
in other words,
says the stuffed owl
to the fly
which, with a buzz,
is trying with its head
to break through the window-pane.

EO

End of the Game

When the ball had rolled away
and come to a stop
against the black wall of evening,

a little boy,
a fat little boy,
on whom they would put
an owl's head
so that he would improve
the front of the house,

walks through a dark gate
and a gray courtyard,
discovers the ciliary motion
of scattered stones
and broken boards,
watching, out of the corner of his eye,
the old stairs mating in the cellar,
the silent dance of carbon,
the washtub's dry tears,

the little boy,
the fat little boy,
on whom they would put
Punch's head,
so he could nod
and tinkle his bells
at each encounter,

rides on the old spinster tram
and on the train, her
eighty-year-old cousin,
does not spit on the floor
or lean out the window,
does not pull the communication cord
even though he can hear
cries
      for help,
some even crying for help
from inside the earth,
even though he sees

the empty sky,
only slightly outlined with jet planes,

the little boy,
the fat little boy
with his leaking
piggy-bank of a heart

looks out the window
at the world's insane simplicity,
at ruins and new buildings,
at open doors
and closed doors,
at hand-wringing
                    and silence,
yawning mainly from pubs,
the detonating of cobwebs,

he's humming
a fat little song,
conversing
with the house-mouse angel,
opening a compound picture book
of Punches and owls.

Even though he feels
he has a long way to go
to get back
to the future.

Even though he feels it —
like a great word,
like a small round blood-taste
in his mouth —
a wisdom tooth growing,
the tooth
most people
have to have pulled
as they grow old.

DY/MH

Landscape with Poets

Some day when
everything's at rest,
in the curly landscape painted by Rubens
as a background for Baucis and Philemon,

poets will disperse,
in dark capes and hoods,
mute as the silhouettes of milestones,
at five-hundred-yard intervals to the horizon and
    beyond,

and in succession
will strum their electric guitars
and say their verse, strophe, poem,
like a telegram from one stone to another,

in succession,
like automatic keys
on a pipe organ
fingered by monsoon rains,

solitary trees will
hum boskily, sheep
will raise shaggy heads,
Orpheus underground will sound
the upper harmonic registers

and the words that float like clouds,
across the information threshold,
up to the shallow sky,
like proteinoids and oligonucleotides,
words as honest as chemical bonds,
words with the autocatalytic function,
genomic and decoding words,

and there will be
either a new form of life
or, possibly,
nothing.   *DY/DH*

Two in a Landscape

In a bare landscape with dry vineyards,
here and there a mammoth, overgrown with
    newsprint
like scales. A head in front
and another head in the rear. It watches us
intently.

In a wooden shack, our backs against
a rotten door. The trunk approaches
through the gaping window. You protect me with your
    hair's shadow.
I protect you with an indigo whisper.

Nonetheless we come back.
We come back eternally,
head thrown back
against head erect.

Eyeball to eyeball.

DY/MH

The Minotaur's Thoughts on Poetry

Certainly this thing exists. For
on dark nights when, unseen,
I walk through the snail-like windings of the street
the sound of my own roar reaches me
from a great distance.

Yes. This thing exists. For surely
even cicadas were once of gigantic stature
and today you can find mammoths' nests
under a pebble. The earth, of course,
is lighter than it once was.

Besides, evolution is nothing but
a long string of false steps;
and it may happen that a severed head
will sing.

And it's not due, as many believe, to
the invention of words. Blood
in the corners of the mouth is substantially
more ancient and the cores of the rocky planets
are heated by the grinding of teeth.

Certainly this thing exists.
Because
a thousand bulls want to be
human.
And vice versa.

EO

Conversation with a Poet

Are you a poet?
> Yes, I am.

How do you know?
> I've written poems.

If you've written poems it means you *were* a poet. But now?
> I'll write a poem again one day.

In that case maybe you'll be a poet one day. But how will you know it is a poem?
> It will be a poem just like the last one.

Then of course it won't be a poem. A poem is only once and can never be the same a second time.
> I believe it will be just as good.

How can you be sure? Even the quality of a poem is for once only and depends not on you but on circumstances.
> I believe that circumstances will be the same too.

If you believe that then you won't be a poet and never were a poet. What makes you think you are a poet?
> Well — I don't rightly know. And who are you?

EO

The Autumn Orchard

Some pawky,
black apple
executed on a naked twig.

Two pigeons
on a rundown fence
tearing white feathers from themselves
because there's nothing else
worth sorting.

Cinderella has smeared herself
with ashes, trying
to discourage
her father's incest.

Through an open window
a bunch of poets
are cursing violently.

Although, in fact, everything's
just the way they like it.

DY/DH

Literary Bash

Like eggs of hail
from the blue sky,
the buzz of greasy bluebottles,
the twitter of eggheads.

Interior sounds
of matter fatigue.

Never stopping.

But even Orpheus
when things got tougher
and he was leading Eurydice
out of the underworld
was quiet as a grave,
the only sound
his crunching step
on the bodies of snails
shedding indigo blood.

In those days, of course,
there were no
literary bashes.

DY/MH

The Pied Pipers

Dreams have reproduced until
you can't even move in your bed.
And in the library, books give birth to booklets
without any fertilization.

But outside, from the dark, there comes
a kind of tune, as though from ants,
yes, it's coming nearer, maybe a flute,
a catchy melody, sweet, diabetic,
and another and another,

intertwining like an Easter braid,
like snakes, each with two penises,
one with the other in its mandibles,
suggesting that hell and purgatory
and even illegal rubbish dumps
have been shut down,

that instead of information
there's only going to be Truth,

and the lyrical snout of the town
gapes with expectation
and on the gallstone pavements
skinny, grubby, scraggly-bearded
Pied Pipers with backpacks
lead their processions from the river

back,

to the marketplace, to halls, to palaces,
(to cottages), pitiful Pied Pipers,
friends of rats and kids,

it's like the procession
of a whole brigade of underage saviors
(mother waits behind the steering wheel
of night's black limousine),

and it marches to the bed,
it marches into the library,

the truth swelling like a pot of porridge,
long threads of language hang from the Pipers' pipes
like spit, the truth puffs up
like a cuckoo's egg in our homes

and instead of molecular darkness
there's a sudden yellow-brown
as if pus were getting pregnant:

the Pied Pipers' roads in Siebenburgen Land
are lined with boils
that burst, one after the other
while the truth howls and trumpets,
like a dead driver, slumped against his car-horn,

"nothing but" overwhelms us.

Which may be that salvation they've been preaching.

DY/MH

Anatomy of January

On the carpal bones
metacarpal bones with vanishing cartilege,
the ulnar
like a ruler for parakeets.

A string is attached to the joint,
a string that goes over the horizon,
southwest.

Rooks are falling from the sky,
under oath.

DY/MH

The Rain at Night

With mouse-like teeth
the rain gnaws at stone.
The trees parade through the town
like prophets.

Perhaps it's the sobbing
of the monstrous angels of darkness,
perhaps the suppressed laughter
of the flowers out there in the garden,
trying to cure consumption
by rustling.

Perhaps the purring
of the holy drought
under any kind of cover.

An unspeakable time,
when the voice of loudspeakers cracks
and poems
are made not of words
but of drops.

GT

Fog

The last road has fallen.
From every corner of the breathing fields
the triumphant sea draws nearer
and rocks in its waves
and voices of goldfinches
and the voices of the town.

We are a long way
from space and time,
we come upon the bobbing silhouettes
of stray dinosaurs
and the rayed shadows of Martians
who cannot see for fear.

You have something more to say, but
I do not understand you:
between us stretches
the enormous body of reality
and from its severed head
bubble the clots
of white blood.

GT

Behind the House

Behind the house the cracked pots of human fate,
the child's scooter, wise in its old age.
On the clothesline, a cloud of elderly breath.
Nitrogen oxide. A drop of blood.

And in the shed, in a heap,
torn rags, rusted rasps and ratchets, new regrets, old
   quarrels
and angels.

DY/MH

The Earliest Angels

The first angels were swarthy, stooped,
hairy, with sloping foreheads
and crested skulls,
arms down to the knees. In place of wings
they had two parachutes of skin,
a kind of black flying squirrel
in the volcanic winds.

Totally trustworthy.
They performed astounding miracles.
Transubstantions. Metamorphoses
of mud into mudfish.
A rocking horse
inflated to heavenly size,
atomic fusion at room temperature,
holding the mirror up to the spectator,
stirrings of consciousness,
creating the majesty of death.

They worked hard.
They tinkered with graves.
They swam in murky waters.
They huddled in oviducts.
They hid behind the door.
They waited.
        They waited in vain.

DY/MH

Anything About God

On a hill, Cezava,
in the heart of Europe
— the bones of a girl and a young man
from the Bronze Age,
without arms, without feet,
victims of ritual cannibalism.

And here are the varicose veins of the stone,
the last thing they saw
as their thoraxes were being opened,
with torrents of blood,
with a divine roar
and animal defecation.

And here is the vehement, variegated
silence of the soil.

Remarked the master:
Whatever you say about God,
it's wrong.

DY/MH

The Statue of the Master

Inside
not even the twisting
— hair of the Gorgon Medusa —
not even the twisting intestines,

not even the swinging
— a Montgolfier in November —
not even the rising and sinking lungs,

not even the caramel-like
— a silent sweet-shop made of aluminum foil —
not even the caramel brain.

Not even the weight-lifting
— the solid, eternal Atlas —
not even the unremitting heart.

Inside
only stone
and stone
and stone

and it stands in the frost,
lips firmly compressed,

and swallows blood.

DY/MH

The Teaching of the Master

He spoke
and the shirts of penitents
fell to the ground, impregnated.

It was the Caesarian section of thought,
plush dolls were born, jubilating.
It was a profile of Everyman,   .
cut out of black paper.
Ladybugs crawled out from under our fingernails.
Trumpets were heard at the walls of Jericho.
Our genes sizzled.

It was magnificent, as he spoke.
It's just that I can't recall
what he was talking about.

DY/MH

The Last Night Bus

The last night bus echoes away
into the depth
of the night's
spinal cord.

Stars shiver
unless they explode.

There are no other civilizations.
Only the gentle
galactic fear
based on methane.

DY/DH

The Bird

The bird that pecks up seconds.
The bird that swallows minutes.
The bird that digests hours.

The memory bird that restores
to the present
the long-drowned sound of the bell.

The bird trapped in a paper
bag, the bird caught on the bird-lime
of tears, the bird beating its wings
in the deep dungeon of books,

the bird as the slave of letters
which are the slaves of memory,

the bird that wiped out
the landscape's fourth dimension
and twitters now inside the outside,
the little skeleton bird, the brittle
dirty thorax bird,
the bird of matted plumage,
the hangnail bird,

the bird because of whom
there'll never be peace again.

DY/MH

Spacetime

When I grow up and you get small,
then —

(In Kaluza's theory the fifth dimension
is represented as a circle
associated with every point
in spacetime)

— then when I die, I'll never be alive again?
        Never.
Never never?
        Never never.
Yes, but never never never?
        No . . . not never never never,
        just never never.

So we made
a small family contribution
to the quantum problem of eleven-dimensional
   supergravity.

DY/DH